MW00424898

UPPER HUDSON VALLEY BEER

CRAIG GRAVINA & ALAN McLEOD

CHEERS!
CRAIG
GRAVINA

AMERICAN PALATE

Published by American Palate
A Division of The History Press
Charleston, SC 29403
www.historypress.net

Copyright © 2014 by Craig Gravina and Alan McLeod
All rights reserved

Front cover: Albany skyline. *Courtesy of Albert Gnidica.*

First published 2014

Manufactured in the United States

ISBN 978.1.62619.512.7

Library of Congress CIP data applied for.

Notice: The information in this book is true and complete to the best of our knowledge. It is offered without guarantee on the part of the authors or The History Press. The author and The History Press disclaim all liability in connection with the use of this book.

All rights reserved. No part of this book may be reproduced or transmitted in any form whatsoever without prior written permission from the publisher except in the case of brief quotations embodied in critical articles and reviews.

To our wives, neither of whom particularly like beer,
but put up with us anyway.

Contents

ACKNOWLEDGEMENTS

First of all, Craig would like to thank his family (Amy, Zoe and Will) and Alan would like to thank his (Ellen, Abby, David and Annie) for their patience and support.

We would like to thank everyone who contributed to the research and preparation of *Upper Hudson Valley Beer*. Without their help, this book would not have been possible:

The Albany Institute of History & Art, the New Netherland Project, the New York State Library, the New York State Museum, the Metropolitan Museum of Art, Vassar College, "Albany…the Way It Was" Facebook page, Steadfast Beer Company, Beau's All-Natural, Historic Hudson, the Lionheart Pub, C.H. Evans Brewing Company at the Albany Pump Station, Brown's Brewing Company, Tamis Groft, Dr. W. Doulas McCombs, Allison Munsell, Carrie Bernardi, Aaron Nobel, Chris Kobuskie, Robyn Gibson, Viki Weiss, Paul Mercer, Craig Williams, Julie O'Connor, Walter G. Ritchie Jr., Dr. Charles Ghering, Gerry Lorrentz, Chad Fust, Ethan Cox, Ron Pattinson, Martyn Cornell, Carole Osterink, Brian Welch, Aaron Connor, Jordan St. John, Deanna Fox, William S. Newman, Neil Evans, Ryan Demler, Garret Brown, Gregg Stacy, Peter Martin, John Mead, Jerry Aumand, Geoff Huth, Denis Meadows, Dieter Gehring, Colleen Ryan, Eric Hoppel, Jimmy Vielkind, Casey Seiler, Mark Crisafulli, Jeremy Hosier, Steve Beauchesne, Jordan Bamforth, Jennifer Beauchesne, Bob Kay, Chad Polenz and all the members of the Albany Ale Project.

INTRODUCTION

In the spring of 2010, Kingston, Ontario–based beer blogger Alan McLeod stumbled across an advertisement in Newfoundland's *Public Ledger* of October 12, 1847. The ad listed a number of products for sale by Clift, Wood & Co.—coffee, tobacco, candles and Albany ale. What exactly was Albany ale? Shortly thereafter, Craig Gravina, a native of Albany and beer blogger in his own right, had joined Alan in a beery quest for the answer to that question.

The question took them on a journey through the history of New York spanning over four hundred years, from the arrival of the first Dutch explorers to the twenty-first century, and it developed into an international research endeavor dubbed the Albany Ale Project. Nearly five years later, the duo has begun piecing together the history of brewing, not just in Albany, but also the Upper Hudson Valley, laying the foundation to explore the entirety of brewing in New York State and, eventually, the country.

It became clear to the duo, quite early on, that beer does not exist in a bubble, and therefore, an account of its history in the Upper Hudson Valley can't simply be a "story of beer." It has to be a larger narrative than that. It has to be an overall history—a cultural, social and economic history of Albany and the Upper Hudson seen through amber-colored glasses. The success and failure of the brewing industry was directly affected by the world it occupied and still occupies. War, climate, law, ethnicity and a myriad of—what might be considered unrelated—factors in fact give context to the story of Upper Hudson Valley beer.

Although this book delves rather deep into the brewing heritage of the Upper Hudson Valley, it would be impossible to include every brew house and brewery in the nearly seven hundred square miles this book covers. Every hamlet and village between Canajoharie and Hoosick and Saratoga Springs to Kingston most likely had some sort of brewing establishment. But there are simply not enough pages to include them all.

1

THE DUTCH AND NEW NETHERLAND IN THE 1600s

The European newcomers who came from across the Atlantic in the early 1600s had a taste for beer. It should not come as any surprise as all European communities, and especially oceangoing crews, depended on a regular supply of grain-based drinks as a safe and nutritious supply of fluid. Water was simply too unhealthy to rely on. As soon as land was reached, personal or communal ale brewing would have been one of the first activities to be undertaken. With the stabilization of the settlement, personal brewing turned to commercial as small taverns were established, which were in turn followed by larger stand-alone breweries.

Brewing became a cornerstone of society. Some of the families who founded the first commercial breweries in the region passed the skill and wealth created on for generations, turning local indigenous hops and surplus wheat sown for export into small empires and, eventually, political power. Striking an alliance with the Mohawk Nation, the Dutch in the Upper Hudson built themselves security for over four decades until conflict between global empires saw the community pass from Dutch to English control. Rather than be overrun by settlers with other tongues and other customs as might have been expected, the Dutch community was left largely to itself, protected by treaties and accords as well as its relative isolation. As the seventeenth century came to a close, despite dangers from New France to the north, the wheat-brewing culture of the Dutch was expanding in geography and population.

DUTCH DRINKING HABITS IN THE EARLY 1600s

The Dutch who settled the Upper Hudson were drinkers and had been for centuries. The role of beer was central to the culture with brewing processes in the early 1600s not being that different from those of the mid-1400s. The historian Richard Unger describes the years 1450 to 1650 as the golden age of Dutch brewing. In 1600, the citizens of Amsterdam drank an average of over 250 liters of beer annually. Skilled workers and laborers drank more. Sailors in the late 1500s were allotted 4 liters of beer per day. The Dutch brewed with wheat, barley, oats and rye, with wheat being the most prized and therefore most expensive. The taxation of beer was a major source of revenue for the state. Dutch control of northern European shipping trade routes was necessary to protect its need to feed its demand for imported grain brought in from as near as France and as far as the Baltic. Much of that grain was destined for the brewing trade.

THE VOYAGE OF THE *HALF MOON*

In 1609, when the *Half Moon*, commanded by Henry Hudson, entered the mouth of the river that would one day bear his name, it found itself in a busy, populated valley. The river valley and the shores and islands around the mouth were the home to many communities and a number of peoples who spoke a number of related Algonquian languages. They were known as the Lenapes to the south and the Mahicans to the north. The Mahicans named the great river on which they traveled *Mahicanituck* and what would later become Albany was a stronghold.

The diary of Robert Jeut, one of Hudson's crewmen, describes interactions with these local communities that ranged from the murderous to the convivial. On September 20, 1609, Jeut states that Hudson wanted to determine whether the chiefs of the area of Albany had any treachery in them. He gave them so much wine and *aqua vitae* that they were all merry, even though the alcohol was strange to his guests. Two days later, the Mahicans returned with gifts of wampum belts as well as a platter of venison. Things appeared to be going well. On the *Half Moon*'s way south, however, a battle with a community south of the Catskills broke out on October 2, during which the Dutch and English crew killed a number of men with muskets, swords and even a small cannon called a falcon. By the fifth, the *Half Moon* was on the Atlantic Ocean returning to Europe.

The two episodes encapsulated the nature of the cultural clash between the European intruders and the local communities. For almost two centuries to come, conflict as well as alliance marked the relationship between them, as did alcohol. This first meeting introduced the people of the Upper Hudson to strong drink, an aspect of their lives that would be lived there for centuries to come. For better or worse, the session of September 20 was also somewhat ironic for Hudson, who, in 1611, was left to die by his own treacherous men on a desolate Arctic sea. His mutinous crew celebrated their liberation from Hudson by drinking his private store of casked strong ale before dashing back home to England.

Cultural and political clash would follow Hudson's return to Europe as others retraced his route to find the rare woods, minerals and, most importantly, lands fit for the growing of grain. Hudson's voyage was under Dutch patronage and his discoveries bestowed a claim that the Netherlands acted on as part of their throwing off of Spanish rule in the first quarter of the 1600s. At its height, this colony, named *Nieuw-Nederland*, would stretch from southern Delaware to eastern New York. The newly independent Netherlands had recently thrown off the yoke of their Spanish imperial overlords and was entering a century of power based on global trade, naval power and personal as well as commercial liberty. Culturally, the Dutch sat on the north–south border of the beer-wine line as well as on the Catholic-Protestant divide. Their adventures in the western hemisphere built on their control of the Baltic shipping trade and their reach from Indonesia to the Caribbean. They were building an empire that would last until the mid-1900s.

1620s and 1630s

Development of the Hudson by the Dutch did not happen all at once. The short-lived New Netherland Company sought to create a foothold by the establishment of Fort Nassau near Albany on an island a few leagues south of the place where the Mohawk River joined the Hudson. Its more successful rival, the West India Company, gained a charter for trade and colonization of the region in 1621. Conflicting interests between two goals—the promotion of the fur trade with existing nations native to the valley or repopulation with European farmers—would impact the efforts of the West India Company. In addition to provisioning the fur traders, however, the opportunity to replace the nation's dependency on foreign imports of staples, including wheat, was too great to ignore. In 1624–25, ships loaded with livestock, tools, settlers and seed

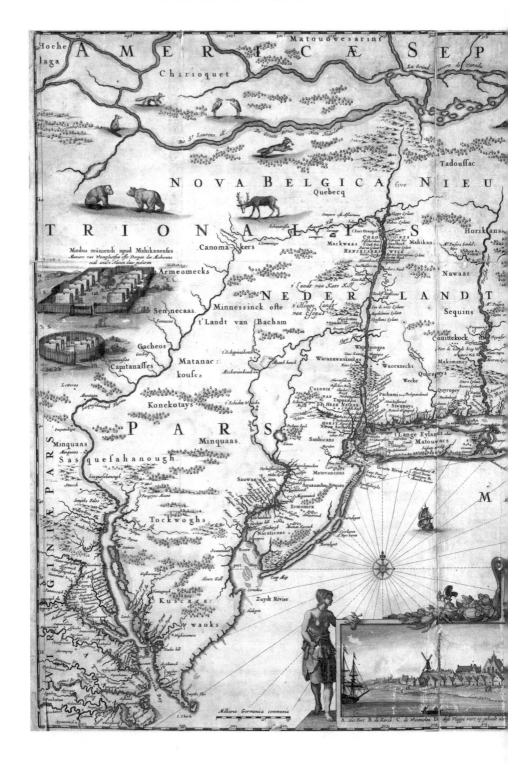

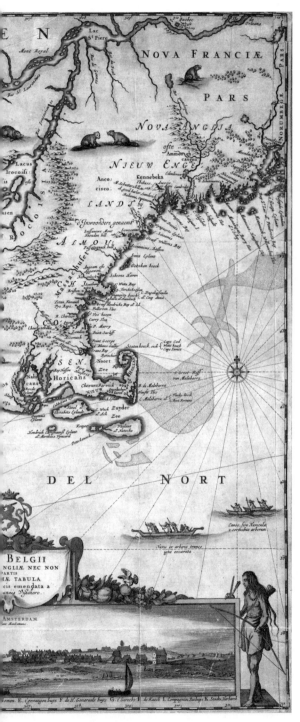

left the Netherlands to cross the ocean for the new lands.

Success did not come immediately. In the fall of 1626, the *Wapen van Amsterdam* returned to the Netherlands with a cargo of unusual plants, rare woods and valuable furs. In 1627, returning ships conveyed many colonists abandoning the project. The plan for settlement was too restrictive, too focused on the fur trade. Colonists were at first barred from competing with trades established in the Netherlands, like weaving. A group of the directors of the West India Company led by Kiliaen van Rensselaer advocated that the success of the colony depended on private investment as well as allowing the colonists the freedom to maximize their own fortunes through the pursuit of individual production. The two sides of the dispute would affect development of New Netherland at Albany for decades.

From their initial settlement in New Amsterdam (now Manhattan) in 1613, the Dutch laid claim to most of what is modern Delaware, Connecticut, New Jersey, New Hampshire, Vermont, parts of Massachusetts, Pennsylvania and Rhode Island, as well as all of New York. *Courtesy of the New York State Library, Manuscripts & Special Collections.*

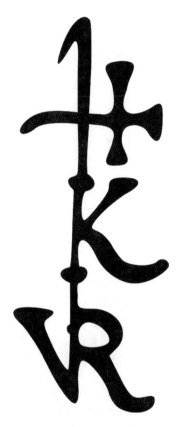

The merchant mark of Kilean van Rensselaer. *Public domain image.*

Van Rensselaer also faced the reality that the colony was not becoming populated with his own countrymen. Many languages, nationalities and races were represented in the settlers. What they had in common was the desire for adventure and advantage. One study has suggested that only 50 percent of colonists were originally from the Netherlands. The rest were a mix of northwestern Europeans. The mixed population brought with it a northern European taste for beer that was fed by trade and familiar with both imported beers as well as local variants. It is also reasonable to expect that they would have been used to the upper end of consumption levels that have been explored by the historian Richard Unger.

The most successful of the settlements in the young colony developed roughly 150 miles north of the mouth of the Hudson River. It sat near the farthest point of Henry Hudson's explorations, just south of where it is joined by its tributary the Mohawk River at what is now Albany, New York. Fort Orange was built where the rivers met as a small outpost and trading site in 1624. The fort—and all its initial thirty inhabitants—fell under the control of the West India Company–appointed director general of the New Netherland colony. They were not alone, as surrounding the fort on all sides for twenty-four square miles was the patroonship of Rensselaerwijck. Its inhabitants, materials and businesses fell under the separate authority of one single man, the patroon Kiliaen van Rensselaer. Within that zone, certain free colonists were able to exploit resources and trade more as they saw fit compared to those in the fort.

In response to attacks from Algonquian nations, the Dutch formed an alliance with a more northwestern people, the Mohawk Nation, which had defeated its neighbors the Mahicans in 1628. They formed an alliance with the colonial Dutch that provided relative peace locally as well as secure access to the hinterland of the continent that would rival other routes controlled by France and Spain. As this alliance grew in strength and trust, by the early 1630s, Kiliaen van Rensselaer acted on his own belief, and the large groups of Dutch settlers began traveling up the Hudson. With their arrival, tensions between the West India Company director general and the patroon grew, due in large part to different goals and uncertain limits of authority.

Despite the clear generosity of life afforded the local inhabitants, the grain-growing, malting and brewing capacity of the Dutch in the Upper Hudson appears to have been greater than simply what was needed to supply local demand. The Albany area was a huge supplier of grain—primarily wheat—and was being developed as a breadbasket supplying New Netherland as well as Dutch interests elsewhere. The colony exported wheat back to the homeland as early as 1626.

From the 1630s, breweries were built to take advantage of this supply. These were not settlers simply making beer for personal consumption, either. This more formal brewing was in addition to household brewing, and all were both regulated and taxed. The first individual to brew in Rensselaerwijck under the authority of the patroon Van Rensselaer was Jacob Albertsen Planck, who was authorized in 1632 "at his own expense and risk and full charge…[to] brew beer to be sold to the men of the Company or to the savages, or do otherwise therewith as he shall think fit."

With the establishment of licensed formal commercial breweries, the colony both founded a commercial industry and provided itself with another level of self-sufficiency and security.

1640s AND 1650s

Within a few years, a greater number of details related to brewing are recorded. In 1643, the patroon Van Rensselaer contracted Evert Pels to work as a public brewer for six years between 1643 and 1649. He located at what would become the colonial brewery in Greenbush. Pels had recently arrived in the colony on the ship *Houttuyn* and traveled in the company of a Reverend Megapolensis and family, a surgeon named Abraham Staes and other farmers and farm-servants. The ship carried a great volume of supplies for the colony, including four thousand tiles and thirty thousand stone for building. It also carried between two hundred and three thousand bushels of malt for the brewery of Mr. Pels. The outpost was well on its way to becoming a complete community.

Commercial brewing soon expanded. Cornelis Cornelisz and Jan Witmont, William Brouwer and Cornelis van Nes and Jan Oothout all operated breweries across the river in Greenbush, while Jacob Hevick and Harmen Hermanse van Gansevoort owned breweries to the south of modern Albany, near the Normanskill, in what is now the town of Bethlehem.

Tensions within the new community affected the trade in beer. In 1644, new regulations on the brewing industry were imposed. Willem Kieft had become the director general of the West India Company in 1638 and enforced a severe rule that undermined the stability of the region. He ordered the massacre of 120 Lenapes on February 25, 1643. He also imposed unauthorized taxation on many products, including beer. When faced with protests, he declared, "I have more power here than the Company itself; therefore I may do and suffer in this country what I please. I am my own master."

He ordered that an excise duty of two guilders be paid on every barrel of beer tapped in the colony. Half was paid by the brewer and half by the tavern owner. In addition to this excise duty, brewers were required to report on the volume of beer that they brewed. When brewers protested and refused to obey the new local rules, beer was confiscated and given to soldiers.

Krieft was replaced after just a few years for putting the entire colonial project at such peril due to his harsh rule and rash risk taking. His replacement at the West India Company, the better-known Peter Stuyvesant, lasted almost two decades and oversaw the physical and economic growth of New Netherland.

Administration of the separate neighboring patroonship continued. Even though Kiliaen van Rensselaer had died in 1643 and was replaced by his son Johan living in Amsterdam, the patroonship was no longer an immediate threat to the power of the new director general. During the first years of Stuyvestant's administration, tensions with the community's own growing local population just beyond the walls of the fort were a greater concern. Nearly one hundred illegal structures had been built directly around the walls of the fort. Stuyesant at first threatened to destroy the shantytown but then decided to establish a permanent village. The center of this new settlement would lie nearly a half mile north of the fort, at the intersection of what Stuyvesant would name Jonkers and Haendlers Streets. That village—named *Beverwijck*—and those two streets, now State and Broadway in downtown Albany, would become a center of the North American brewing world for well over two hundred years.

The plan to create a civic settlement near the fort and therefore beyond the control of the patroon was a success. To serve that settlement, two

Peter Stuyvesant, circa 1660. *Courtesy of the New York Historical Society.*

breweries were soon established in Beverwijk. The brewery on Broadway between what is now Hudson and Division Streets had a rather long lifespan. It was operated first by Pieter Bronck in 1645 and then by Jacob Hevick and Reyndert Pieterszto. Harmen Hermanse and Jan Harmenz Weendorp rented it. The brewery off the Ruttenkill or Rat Creek on State Street between South Pearl and Green Streets didn't fair so well. Opened in 1649, Rutger Jacobsz and Goosen Gerritsz operated it on Jacobsz's property, but in 1657, Jacobsz tore it down and sold the land to Harman Vedder. Beginning in 1647, a small brewery was even operated within the walls of Fort Orange by Jan Labatie. There is no record of Labatie brewing past the mid-1650s. There are mentions of other breweries in the Fort, but none by name or owner. These may have been home-based, noncommercial breweries.

Brewing in both Beverwijk as well as in the patroonship prospered. Brewers became persons of property as well as authority within the colonial administration. Rutger Jacobsz was a magistrate in Rensselaerswyck from 1648 to at least as late as 1662. In addition to owning his own vessel on the river, in 1649, Jacobsz and his partner, Goosen Gerrittsz, rented the patroon's brewery for an annual rent of 450 guilders as well as another guilder for every ton of beer they brewed. In their first year of operation, that extra payment added up to an additional 330 guilders in rent. In 1650, the two men also produced 1,500 *schepels* of malt. A *schepel* was a measure of grain that equaled about three quarters of a bushel, or around twenty-five liters.

By the late 1640s, brewing in Beverwijck was a significant industry, and beer was becoming a problem. In 1648, an ordinance was passed to regulate the sale of beer, wine and brandy within the whole of the colony. Measures were taken to prevent fights and establish operating hours for taphouses on the Sabbath. Among these regulations was also a rule enforcing the separation of the innkeeper—or "tapper"—from the brewer. Brewers were forbidden to tap their own beer, and the tappers were not allowed to brew.

The law was applied against Swedish-born Pieter Bronck. He was the younger brother of Jonas Bronck, for whom the New York City borough of the Bronx is named. Peter Bronck was forbidden to tap beer in 1655 but defied the law. A brewer by trade, Bronck and his wife also ran a tavern in Beverwijck. This prohibition caused Bronck significant monetary loss. A number of attempts to sell his brewery failed. The Swede remained in debt until he finally sold the brewery and the land it sat on to Jacob Hevick in 1661.

Due to distance and local control, such regulations were not established by the ruling parties back in the Netherlands but rather were passed within the local settlement. As masters of an industrial process, brewers became and needed to be wealthy. And with wealth came power. Like many elements of Beverwijck culture, customs from the Dutch Republic were brought to New Netherland. One of these customs was the establishment of a *vroedschap*, a city council made up of established men in the city. From its ranks, the colony's magistrates were chosen. Goosen Gerritsz van Schaick was one of these early brewers who served on council and also as a magistrate. The capacity to secure the commercial interests of established brewers was assured.

Pieter Bronck had a contentious relationship with the *vroedschap*. During the 1650s, Bronck was enjoined from tapping strong beer due to not paying the proper excise tax. Bronck was caught, most likely because he was also operating a tavern while brewing—another violation. Bronck moved his family to what is now Greene County. His house (pictured here) still stands as a museum. *Public domain image.*

Separate from the control of the patroon, the area directly in and around Beverwijck had by far the greatest density of breweries—twelve at its height, with eight surviving into the 1650s. One, Franz Barensten Pastoor, established a brewery on Broadway near Maiden Lane in 1653. Jan Dircksz van Eps also brewed there until he resettled in Schenectady in the 1660s. Unfortunately, Van Eps was killed in the 1690 massacre there when the French and their aboriginal allies swept down from the north. The brewery site at Beverwijck, however, would remain a brewery until being sold in 1736 to be used as a parsonage.

Dean Street is a courtyard now, but in 1654, it is where partners Pieter Hartgers, Volkert Janse Douw and Jan Thomase built their brewery. This is the site of the "Old Post Office" building today. Ownership would later transfer to Goosen Gerritsz, a fur trader, brewer and longtime resident of Beverwijck. After Gerritsz's death in 1679, his wife sold half the brewery to Sybant van Schaick, Gerritsz's son who had been operating the brewery. Sybant would die young, at the age of thirty in 1686. Sybant's younger brother Anthony would assume control of the brewery but then capitalized more on the success of his father-in-law, Teunis Cornelisse, a prominent businessman and politician. There is no mention of a brewery in Van Schaick's will, written in January 1737.

The brewery on Beaver Street between South Pearl and Green Streets backing up to the Ruttenkill had a short, tough life. Jacob Janz van Noortsrant originally purchased the land and built a brewery. Rutger Jacobsz bought the property in 1654 and brewed there until he sold off his brewing equipment and closed shop in 1662.

Harmen Harmanse immigrated to New Netherland in the 1650s and opened a small brewery south of Fort Orange. He married Maria Conyn, the daughter of Leendert Conyn, a very early Beverwijck brewer. Moving to the village, he and Jan Harmenz Weendorp would rent the Bronck Brewery and, shortly thereafter, Hermanse would purchase his own brewery at the southeast corner of Market Street—now Broadway—and Maiden Lane. This is the future site of another well-known Albany landmark, the Stanwix Hall Hotel. Harman's only surviving son, Leendert Gansevoort, would continue the family business, prospering into the early eighteenth century. The brewery would become the center of his property, which extended from Market Street east down to the shore of the river. By the early 1700s, the Gansevoort family had become part of the city's commercial elite.

1660s and 1670s

The first patroon to actually live permanently in the colony was Jeremias van Renssealer, son of Kiliean, who built a series of mills as well as a brew house to the west of his manor near the mouth of what is now known as Patroon Creek on the Hudson River in the early 1660s. It is unclear if this was a commercial brewery or one operated for those on the patroon's estate.

The pleasures and freedoms of Dutch life in the Hudson Valley in the mid-1600s were described in the journal of Englishman Daniel Denton, who included observations on the role of beer in Dutch culture:

> *Here those which Fortune hath frowned upon in England, to deny them an inheritance amongst their brethren, or such as by their utmost labors*

can scarcely procure a living—I say such may procure here inheritances of lands and possessions, stock themselves with all sorts of cattle, enjoy the benefit of them whilst they live, and leave them to the benefit of their children when they die. Here you need not trouble the shambles for meat, nor bakers and brewers for beer and bread, nor run to a linen-draper for a supply, everyone making their own linen and a great part of their woolen cloth for their ordinary wearing.

The distinction between commercial brewing and household production was clear. Brewing capacity was subject to local regulation over the retail sale of beer, but "private individuals were allowed the privilege to brew whatever quantity of beer they might require for consumption in their own families." The reason was perhaps due to the abundance of local ingredients. Grain crops—and wheat in particular—were so plentiful there were usually surpluses for home malting. Hops grew wild in the woods.

In August 1664, the growing might of the English Royal Navy made itself known to Dutch administration and residents when four frigates sailed into the harbor off the island of Manhattan and and demanded the surrender of the entire colony. With that, New Netherland director general Peter Stuyvesant acquiesced. Dutch New Amsterdam became British New York. The colony would fall back into Dutch hands briefly in 1673, but by 1674 it was back under British control, where it would stay for a century.

Beverwijck was renamed Albany in honor of Prince James, Duke of Albany, later James II of England, and its street names were anglicized—Jonkers Street became State Street, Handlers Street became Market Street and later Broadway. With the English rule came English law, and in the Duke of York's Laws of 1665, special provisions for brewing were set out:

That no person whatsoever shall henceforth undertake the Calling or work of Brewing Beer for Sale, but only such as are known to have Sufficient Skill and knowledge in the art or Mistery [sic] of a Brewer, That if any undertake for victualling of Ships or other Vessels or Master or owner of any such Vessels or any other person shall make it appear that any Beer bought of any person within this Government do prove unfit, unwholesome and useless for their supply, either through the insufficiency of the Mault or Brewing or unwholesome Cask, the Person wronged thereby, shall be and is hereby enabled to recover equal & Sufficient damage by Action against that Person that put the Beer to Sale.

Although this watercolor was painted in the Netherlands, Adriaen van Ostade's 1680 *Tavern Interior* is also representative of the boisterous atmosphere within a New Netherland tavern. Taverns were often prohibited from brewing their own beer under Dutch control; however, British regulation on tavern-brewed beer was far less restrictive. *Courtesy of the Musée Royaux des Beaux-Arts, Brussels, Belgium.*

Cultural conflict arose with the British takeover. The Dutch became the butt of English jokes implying that New Netherlanders were cheap and lazy. Some New Netherlanders were actually sold into slavery and sent to the southern British colonies in Virginia and the Carolinas. However, one last negotiation by Stuyvesant made a huge difference to those Dutch living in the Hudson Valley. Article VII of the Articles of Transfer protected their religious freedom. While the British almost everywhere else in the colony ignored those freedoms granted, in Albany at the northern most end of the Hudson River, it secured their cultural autonomy.

As part of the life of the community, commercial brewing continued under British rule. The brewery operated first by Pieter Bronck was sold to Albertus Janse Rijckman in 1678. Albert Rijckman, or Ryckman, would become arguably the most prominent brewer in Beverwijck of the late 1600s. Albert's son Harmanusthen assumed control of the brewery at the turn of the eighteenth century and ran it until his own death in 1755.

As a personal estate, expansion of the *patoonship* also continued under the new administration based in England. A year after the English took control of all of New Netherland, Arent van Curler, cousin to Kilean van Rensselaer, led a group of settlers and established a village fifteen miles northwest of Beverwijck. The new settlement sat on the southern bank of the Mohawk River, near its confluence with the Hudson. It was named *Schaenhectede* and sat just to the north the Rensselaerwijck border. Many of the early settlers and brewers of this new community came from Beverwijck and the surrounding area. Philip de Brouwer relocated from Beverwijck in 1662, reestablished his business and continued to brew—with his apprentice Jan Pootman—in Schenectady until his death in 1668. Adam Vrooman, Jan Dircksz van Eps and Jacob Janse Schermerhorn, all one-time Beverwijck brewers, migrated to the new village.

THE 1680s AND 1690s

Local control of life in the community was further enhanced in 1686, when Albany was granted its own municipal charter by colonial governor of the province of New York, Thomas Dongan, Second Earl of Limerick. The Dongan Charter separated Albany formally from the outlying lands of the patroon in Rensselaerswijck and established the community as a city. It provided local municipal control over a wide range of matters, including specifically the sale of beer and the operation of taverns. It created a council of aldermen and provided the new city with municipal control over trade in the district, importantly including all trade with neighboring Native American nations. Leading citizens associated with brewing families like the Van Schaicks and the Gansevoorts were granted influential positions under the new local government.

Acting together, the Articles of Transfer from the 1660s and the Dongan Charter of 1686 served as cornerstones of both religious freedom and political autonomy that allowed Albany to continue to exist and grown as a distinct society within greater English colonial life. The Dutch Reform Church continued to operate in the colony, and the leading brewing families continued to participate in both government and commercial success—all conducted mainly in Dutch. Language affects culture. Had the English quelled the Dutch church, New York as a whole may have adopted new aspects of their overlords' culture sooner. Instead, Dutch culture thrived well into the second half of the eighteenth century with echoes continuing well beyond it.

As illustration of stability and continuity, by the late 1600s, Albany began to see a new generation of North American–born brewers emerge. For example, at some point during the 1680s, Beverwijck-born Bastian Harmanse would open a brewery along Market Street. Unfortunately, the exact location of that brewery is unknown. Harmanse's son, Teunis Visscher, joined the family business, learning the trade from his father, and would run his family brewery on Market Street for more than fifty years.

As might be expected in a relatively organized colonial community, the map shows that even as early as the seventeenth century, there were demarcated brewing zones in Albany. The success of the breweries depended on taking advantage of local resources and access to good brewing water. The two breweries to the west along the Ruttenkill closed within a short period of time. The brewery in the fort didn't fare much better. The other four breweries on the east side of Broadway in the heart of the village, by contrast, thrived for decades. In the case of the Gansevoorts, they continued brewing for well over a century. It is fairly easy to see why those breweries along Broadway survived: access to the river. The river provided clear, clean water year round as well as easy transportation to and from the village. The breweries along Broadway had easy access to the waterfront while the more westerly breweries along the Ruttenkill had to move their beer across the village to access the wharf. Also, even in the driest of seasons, the Hudson River was not going to run dry. The smaller creeks might have gone brackish or fully dry in some years. The brewery in the fort didn't have the support that the surrounding population in the village supplied. Like the Ruttenkill breweries, the brewer in Fort Orange failed fairly quickly.

In addition to the location of the breweries, their sheer number is intriguing. A minimum of twelve breweries operated in Beverwijck alone—twelve breweries to supply, at maximum, one thousand people. That seems a bit much. The first patroon himself gave a possible clue for the proliferation of breweries in an early letter. Writing in 1632, Kiliaen van Rensselaer stated, "As soon as there is a supply of grain on, I intend to erect a brewery to provide all New Netherland with beer."

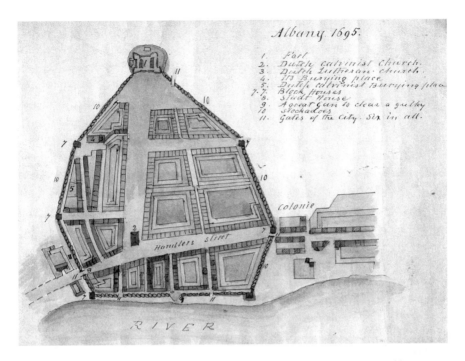

During the 1660s, palisades surrounded Beverwijck; by the 1690s, it was enclosed by a defensive stockade. In the late 1670s, Fort Orange was abandoned, and Fort Frederick was built within the stockade walls. The city's easternmost wall hugged the river's shoreline, allowing easy access to the water via two gates, north and south. Many of the city's early breweries were located along Handlers Street, which also paralleled the river. *Courtesy of the Albany Institute of History and Art.*

It is compelling to imagine that the twin communities of the patroon at Rensselaerwijck and the West India Company at Beverwijck may have been established in part to supply beer to the whole of New Netherland and perhaps other parts of the global Dutch empire. It was not as farfetched as it might seem, as Albany would supply distant drinkers under the protection of another empire two hundred years later. There has not as yet, however, been sufficient data uncovered to definitively confirm this possibility.

Near the end of the century, the stability that had helped the colony grow was broken, as the community suffered an attack that would foreshadow the century of conflict to come. The winter of 1690 brought terror to the tiny western outpost of Schaenhectede. England was at war with France and the warfare had spilled over into the new world. In the predawn hours of February 8, a raiding party of French Canadians as well as Ironquois and Algonquian allies launched an attack on the slumbering residents of

Schenectady in retribution for a massacre of French settlers in 1689 at Montreal. The raids carried out were part of the King William's War, one of a number of colonial conflicts between the British and French.

By the dawn, with the village burning, sixty settlers—men, women and children—were dead and many others captured. Jan Dircksz van Eps, Jan Pootman and Andries Arentse Bratt were among those killed. Andreis Bratt's parents and uncle were early Norwegian settlers of Beverwijck. Born there in 1653, Bratt came to Schenectady with his family in 1662 at the age of twelve. By the 1670s, he had established a brewery there on a lot between what is now Washington Avenue and Union, State and Church Streets. It was outside that brewery that he was killed during the 1690 massacre. His son Arent Bratt survived the attack and, when he grew old enough, assumed ownership of his father's brewery, operating it until his death in 1765.

Another brewing family was caught up in the massacre and aftermath. Born in the Netherlands, Adam Vrooman came to Beverwijck with his family in the 1650s. At the age of twenty-one, Vrooman indentured himself to Cornelius Vanden Burgh, a local millwright, to learn the trade. By 1683, he had built his own mill along the Sandkill Creek in Schenectady. Vrooman survived the 1690 attack, but his sons, Wouter and Barent, as well as his brother Jan and his cousin Matthys Meese were all captured and taken as prisoners north to New France. Voorman rebuilt his life and business, and in 1697, he even traveled north and successfully bartered for his relatives' release. With the family returned to Schenectady, Vrooman began growing his milling business and expanded into brewing.

Conclusion

Despite being caught up in larger conflicts with both the English and the French empires for most of its existence, the Dutch society established in the Upper Hudson hung on and expanded. As the brewing families of the Upper Hudson were becoming established leaders in the community, the community's export wealth based on wheat continued to supply a beer-drinking culture that had largely separated itself from the old motherland. Through a combination of isolation, wealth and security, the Dutch in America were slowly becoming Dutch Americans.

2

COLONIAL-ERA BREWING

LOCAL WATER, WHEAT MALT AND DUTCH HOPS

A s brewing in the northern frontier of New Netherland progressed from rustic personal ale making to tavern brewing to small-scale, stand-alone commercial production, brewers were required and also able to rely on local resources as well as a mix of traditional and inventive techniques.

In some English colonial settings, much of the work of brewing was assigned to women in the home, but that was not necessarily the case in Dutch culture. The historian Unger shows that even in the 1500s, commercial brewing in the Netherlands included both wage-earning women and men. Also, in its upper reaches, New Netherland was not settled originally as a balanced society, leaving an excess of men, whether soldiers, laborers or traders. As was seen on the Newfoundland coast and in Hudson Bay in the 1600s, however, men at the edge of an empire's reach were able to capably brew their own beer for their pleasure and good health.

LOCAL WATER

We have seen that what is now the city of Albany was first settled on a river near where it is joined by a tributary reaching westward into the continent. These rivers can be traced, as can the paths of the three Albany creeks: Beaverkill, or Beaver Creek, to the south; Ruttenkill in the middle; and Fox Creek to the north to form an understanding for the purpose of the community for most of its existence. Albany is a seaport that is located 150 miles into the heartland and set at the mouth of the Mohawk, a circumstance that made it the key to the route for the expansion of Albany County to the west until the 1770s, when new counties were carved from its edges.

The first Dutch settlers embraced the great waterway that they called the North River. They relied on it for transportation north, nearly to Lake George in the Adirondack Mountains; south to it is mouth at the island of Manhattan; and on into the Atlantic Ocean. In addition to transportation in this time before the advent of well drilling, the river provided clean, unpolluted water. While now one can expect brewers to manage the fine points of water composition, it is the abundance and cleanliness of the water in the 1600s that made the development of brewing possible in this little frontier village. The river also afforded convenience. Those early breweries located along the Ruttenkill, farther from the river, fared far worse than those along its waterfront.

WHEAT MALT

The diary of English traveler Daniel Denton published in 1670 confirms the brewing of wheat ale in his description of the wide-ranging drinking habits of the Dutch population of the Hudson:

> *Their best Liquors are Fiall, Passado, and Madera Wines, the former* [of which] *are sweetish, the latter a palish Claret, very spritely and generous, two shillings a Bottle; their best Ale is made of Wheat Malt, brought from Sopus and Albany about threescore Miles from New-York by water; Syder twelve shillings the barrel; their quaffing liquors are Rum-Punch and Brandy-punch, not compounded and adulterated as in England, but pure water and pure Nants.*

The scale of wheat ale brewing must have been significant as in 1649 a legal ordinance barring brewing with wheat was passed apparently in response to a crop collapse. Brewing with wheat made sense given, as noted earlier, the region surrounding what is now Albany served as a breadbasket for the entire New Netherland area. In 1655, a description of agriculture in the Hudson Valley reported that wheat was grown in far greater proportions compared to the barley crop then grown back in the Netherlands.

The preference for wheat continued into the eighteenth century. In 1749, the scale of wheat production in the Upper Hudson and Mohawk River Valleys was described by Peter Kalm, a professor from a Swedish university who toured eastern North America from 1748 to 1750 and prepared a survey of economic and natural resources. He made these notes on June 15, 1749, that the wheat crop around Albany was a great success with as much as a twenty-to-one return on the sown seed. Rye was also sown, but not much barley was planted, as it was unprofitable. Significantly, he noted that they malted wheat.

During the precolonial period, not only was wheat the grain crop best suited in the Upper Hudson for local purposes, but by the late 1600s, it also fed a growing export trade into the West Indies market, including to the Dutch islands. The malting of wheat and brewing of wheat beer likely resulted from what was almost a monoculture in a controlled agricultural economy. Given both the West India Company and the Duke of York had discouraged freehold farming, this focus on wheat was likely part of a command economy as much as market forces.

HUDSON VALLEY HOPS

While the primary goal of the settlement of the Hudson Valley was the development of an agricultural colony, not all crops were given equal opportunity. Author Oliver Rink has described how from the outset of colonization the relocation of Dutch farming techniques and resources were provided for in the "Instructions from the Company to the Director-General":

> While the Oranje Boom languished at Plymouth, the main body of the expedition sailed from the Zuider Zee in a four ship squadron under the command of Willem Verhulst. Verhulst's instructions have survived, and they confirm the Company's intention to establish a permanent agricultural colony in New Netherland. The commander was under orders to Transport to New Netherland "divers trees, vines, and all sorts of seeds" and to have them planted and sown in their proper season.

The instructions to the first director general go on to make very specific guidance on how to manage the vineyard to make raisins, wine or even brandy. There is no reference to hops in the instructions. By the 1640s, however, hops are significant enough a crop that the author Jan Folkerts remarked that hops were present if not successful—unlike the bountiful wheat, the leading crop in the patroonship. Hops also are described in at least one contract in the 1640s as part of a transaction. In 1642, David Pietersz de Vries recorded that "our Netherlanders can…can brew as good a beer here as in our Fatherland, for good hops grow in the woods."

The legacy of the Dutch appreciation for these local native hops continues. While the rivers and creeks have been compromised by centuries of urban growth and industrialization and while the breadbasket of the nation has moved far to the west, the hops are still there, at least in the form of a likely descendant. The hop Cluster was a key early commercial hop that is the genetic ancestor of many of the great American hops today. Wild hops still grow in and around the hills surrounding Albany, including some on farms that have remained in the hands of Dutch settler families.

How Did They Brew?

As with many mundane tasks, descriptions of the techniques of early brewing in the Upper Hudson are few and far between. The greatest puzzle is how they dealt with all that wheat. Unlike barley, the husk of a grain of wheat does not lead to a porous mass in the mash, a critical point in the brewing process. Wheat tends to get "stuck" or form a thick porridge that is resistant to the lautering stage of beer making, during which the sweet sugars that are created by the mass are rinsed away from the grain. A clue to a key technique that may have been used is found in the 1803 diary of Lord Selkirk, who was traveling through western New York when he noted the scene at a frontier brewery at what is now Geneva, New York:

> *Half barley half wheat he uses about 500 Bushels of barley vis all that he can find to buy & pays the price of wheat—being very little cultivated… Wheat alone makes thick stuff & the liquor will not run of from the grain—sometimes by the assistance of a mixture of Chopt straw it can be done, but the wheat at any rate does not improve the quality of the beer.*

By the time Selkirk wrote this entry to his diary, straw cutting was an old trade nearing the end of its time. Cut straw was a handy item used as fodder, stuffing and, apparently, the loosening material for wheat mash to make beer. It could well be that the malt was kilned over straw as well to ensure it stayed as pale as possible.

Conclusion

For a culture with a long beer-drinking tradition, the Dutch population of the 1600s and 1700s in the Upper Hudson Valley could not have found a better new home. Unlike the Dutch settlers' overpopulated homeland, the region freely gave them the water, hops and wheat they needed to make the beer their culture depended on. Along with the political autonomy, use of local resources created a local form of strong wheat beer that found favor as long as its brewing lasted. Unfortunately, both the exact procedure of ale making and the experience of the ale-drinking colonists remain today somewhat mysterious.

3

BRITISH ALBANY FROM THE 1660s TO 1800

BUILDING ON THE DUTCH LEGACY OF THE 1600s

The legacy of those early Dutch brewers was felt for many decades after their, or their breweries, deaths. The twin protections of the Articles of Transfer and the Dongan Charter provided the stability that allowed the community in the Upper Hudson Valley to continue on its own cultural and political path. Economically, the grain farms established in the region in the 1600s would be built on and help the area become by the 1750s not only the breadbasket of New York but also a supplier of grain for colonial America, as well as for elsewhere in the world. In fact, the Upper Hudson, as well as its tributaries in the Schoharie and Mohawk Valleys, became so crucial for feeding the Continental army during the American War for Independence that British raiding parties burned its farms and settlements, hoping to starve the insurrectionist into submission or at least keep them at bay.

Like grain production, New York's hops industry would grow from the roots of the early Dutch settlers. Varieties that date from the Dutch era were hybridized and bred with indigenous species in New York, and these formed the basis for an explosion of hops production in New York State during the middle and late nineteenth century. The first commercial hops farm in New York was established in 1808; within fifteen years, eleven counties in central New York would be producing hops for commercial purposes. By midcentury, the state was growing 90 percent of the United States' hops crop and exporting it around the globe.

It is most likely that a range of strengths of beer was brewed, but there seems to be a historical connection between strong beer and the Albany area. Strong beer was common in the Dutch Republic. According to beer historian Ron Pattinson, the grain bill for a 1515 dubbel koyt, an oat-based gruit from the town of Zutphen in the Netherlands, results in an eighteen-degree Plato brew, or over 7 percent alcohol. It stands to reason that the Beverwijck brewers would have brewed at least some of their beer to a similar strength. By the turn of the nineteenth century, "Albany Strong Beer" was being advertised. Within forty years, the dynamo double-strength XX Albany ale, estimated to be at least between 7 and 9 percent alcohol by volume, would be brewed across the city and exported outside the nation. That tradition of strong beer brewing starts with the brewers of Beverwijck, and that tradition is followed by the brewers of Albany until the late 1800s.

More importantly, the establishment of Beverwijck as a brewing hub so early on in the history of the United States set the area up to become one of North America's brewing capitals 150 years later. Once the breweries were established in the 1600s, the industry simply expanded through the first two-thirds of the 1700s. With trade routes west on the Mohawk and south on the Hudson, distribution was far easier than for those settlements with only one access point. The ancestors of those early Dutch brewers—the Van Schaicks, Ryckmans, Gansevoorts—would continue brewing throughout the eighteenth century, strengthening the city's bond to beer. These families would also continue the *vroedschap* tradition, serving as pillars of the Albany community, influential businessmen, local civic leaders, state and federal representatives and military heroes. The notion of the Albany politician/brewer would, in fact, continue well into the twentieth century. Albany political boss and head of its Democratic party from 1919 until his death in 1977, Daniel O'Connell purchased Hedrick Brewing just after the repeal of national Prohibition in 1933. That brewery operated into the mid-1960s.

1700–1750s

The role of beer in the culture of Albany at the outset of the 1700s can be seen in two church events at the turn of the eighteenth century. On February 15, 1700, one of the church's poor died. She was Ryseck, the widow of Gerrit Swart. The records of the *onkosten*, or expenses for the burial and ceremony borne by the community, have been retained. There were more than a few expenses in addition to the cost of the coffin and the fee paid Hendrick Roseboom, the *doodgraver*. In addition to 150 sugar cakes and sufficient tobacco and pipes, six gallons of Madeira were provided, along with one of rum. In addition, twenty-seven guilders were paid by the congregation for a half vat and an anker of good beer. The event seems to have been a social one. A similar table was set when Jan Huybertse passed away in February 1707. He was one of the *nooddruftige*, or the needy, and church coffers paid out for three gallons of wine and one of rum in addition to paying eighteen guilders for a vat of good beer. In each case, respects were paid by the local believing community with a good send off and a good drink for those in attendance.

These funerals illustrate the continuation of Dutch society well into the British era. Along with other members of the upper strata, old Dutch family breweries, such as the Ryckmans, Gansevoorts, Visschers and Van Schaicks, established in the seventeenth century continued to operate along the Broadway corridor well into the second half of the eighteenth. Brewing may have created wealth and power for these families, and by the end of the eighteenth century, all four had built on their brewing wealth, diversified and become involved in everything from lumber to politics, as often as much with New France in the north as with the British to the south.

The prominent brewer Albert Janse Ryckman was elected mayor of Albany in 1702 after serving for years as an alderman. His house was on the south corner of Hudson Street and Broadway alongside the brewery that sat on the riverfront. His son Harmanus, one of nine children who lived to see adulthood, ran the brewery into the 1750s. Even into the nineteenth century, Ryckman descendants were involved in Albany brewing. Gerrit Ryckman partnered with Lancelot Fidler, later taking the name Howard, and brewed during the 1830s. Albany's Ryckman Avenue is named for the family.

Schenectady's Adam Vrooman, the survivor of the massacre in 1690, purchased the milling rights to all of Sandkill Creek by 1703. In 1710, Vrooman's third son, Wouter, began operating the mill known as Brandywine Mill. In 1718, Vrooman and his second son, Barent, built a brew house on what is now Union Street—sometimes called "Brewer's Street"—where the railway met the canal. In 1724, Jan, the youngest Vrooman, joined his brother and father at the brewery and was given his own lands and brewing equipment a few years later. Adam Vrooman retired in 1726, purchasing 1,400 acres of land farther west into the frontier lands of the Schoharie to build a farm. He died in 1730, but his sons continued to brew for decades more. The geologic formation known as Vroman's Nose near Middleburgh, Schoharie County, New York, is named for Adam Vrooman.

Of all the great Dutch brewing families, the early eighteenth century would see the Gansevoorts become the most influential, elevating themselves

This silver ale tankard was crafted by the New York City silversmith Peter Quintard for Leendert Gansevoort sometime between 1725 and 1750. Its lid is inscribed with Gansevoort's initials, LCG, and the body of the vessel bares the Gansevoort family crest. *Courtesy of the Metropolitan Museum of Art.*

into the elite of New York society. Harmen Harmanse's only surviving son, Leendert Gansevoort, would continue the family business. The brewery stood behind the house, like that of Ryckman, on the riverbank east of Broadway, then known as Market Street. At the end of Maiden Lane, the dock that reached out into the river was known as Gansevoort's wharf. Leendert's son Johannes would continue to grow the brewery after his father's death in 1762. Johannes's brother, Harmen, broadened the family business by opening his merchant's store near the brewery. The Gansevoorts family operated their brewery until 1805, tearing it down and erecting their hotel, Stanwix Hall, named in honor of the fort in what is now Rome, New York, that was defended by family member General Peter Gansevoort during the War for American Independence. The name Gansevoort still lives on as a luxury hotel in New York City, as well as a hamlet in Saratoga County, New York.

Despite Dutch political and cultural autonomy, the British were not taking an entirely hands-off approach to the Hudson Valley. Flour and bread were exported to the West Indies, and from 1702 to 1713, during Queen Anne's War, New York State enjoyed a lucrative market for its wheat in Lisbon courtesy of British trade routes. After 1713, the settlement of the Albany region expanded, with new farms adding to the supply of grain being shipped out to the British Empire as well as the Dutch West Indies. From 1715 to 1723, the population of Albany County doubled. In

1723, then Surveyor General Cadwallader Colden submitted a report to London on the state of New York trade. Wheat was clearly the colony's most important export. In 1737, the population of the county reached ten thousand. Brewers like Ryckman, Vrooman and Gansevoort were supplying the booming population with their hopped beers made of local wheat.

By the 1730s and 1740s, the focus of the fur and pelt trades had migrated west to Oswego on Lake Ontario with control soon shifting away from established Albany merchants to daring newcomers like William Johnson. The established elite Dutch families were enjoying their wealth as suited their tastes. From 1715 to 1745, Albany Dutch merchants commissioned a large number of portraits in a European style, celebrating their domestic and commercial stability. Paintings of the Gansevoort family show men and boys without wigs dressed simply with farms and mills in the background. Dr. Alexander Hamilton, visiting Albany in 1744, found the focus on wealth obsessive: "They spare no pains or trouble to acquire…their whole thoughts being turned upon profit and gain." The lack of literate society was noted as well as the habit of heavy drinking. Hamilton remarks that they were "toapers" and "bumper men" for whom the act of punning was considered to pass for wit.

The Visschers also continued brewing into the eighteenth century. By the 1720s, Bastian Harmanse's son, Teunis Visscher, had joined the family business, learning the trade from his father. Teunis ran his family's brewery on Market Street for more than fifty years. In 1756, Bastian Visscher, Teunis's son, followed in his grandfather's and father's footsteps, but like many of the other early Albany brewers, he began diversifying into other business ventures, most notably construction. Bastian Vissher became a notable revolutionary, advocating for American independence in the 1770s.

Sometime during the 1730s, the Wendell family, relative newcomers to brewing, opened a series of mills and a brew house along the Beverkill Creek, near what is now the basin of Lincoln Park. This area became an Albany landmark simply known as Wendell's Mills and operated almost to the turn of the nineteenth century, although it is unknown if the brewery did as well.

During King George's War of 1744–48, Royal Governor George Clinton was obliged to pursue war efforts against New France. This raised conflict with the Albany merchants, led by James DeLancy, who held strong trade ties with Montreal. Harmen Gansevoort was one of these merchants, taking payments mainly in grain, along with some furs and pelts. Much of the grain may have ended up being brewed into beer by his brother, Johannes. As the

This 1737 painting of Abraham Wendell shows one of the family's mills along the Beverkill in the background. *Courtesy of the Albany Institute of History and Art.*

midcentury passed, the family's fortunes were less and less tied to brewing, even if Johannes had amassed a considerable fortune himself. Among the silverware often acquired as a means to both save and display accumulated wealth, the now elderly patrician Leendert Gansevoort had a silver tankard for his beer that was deeply engraved with the family's coat of arms on its front and his own monogram on the lid. It stayed in the family for five generations until, in 1901, it was placed in the collection of the Metropolitan Museum of Art in New York City.

When Swedish botanist Peter Kalm traveled through both New York and New France around this time, he kept a detailed diary. It was filled with observations on the state of the economy and society in each region. In the region of the Upper Hudson and Albany County, one of the main things he noticed was the wheat:

> *They sow wheat in the neighborhood of Albany, with great advantage. From one bushel they get twelve sometimes; if the soil be good, they get twenty bushels. If their crop amounts only to ten bushels from one, they think it very trifling. The inhabitants of the country round Albany are Dutch and Germans. The Germans live in several great villages, and sow great quantities of wheat, which is brought to Albany and from thence they send many yachts laden with flour to New York. The wheat flour from Albany is reckoned the best in all North America, except that from Sopus or King's town, a place between Albany and New York. All the bread in Albany is made of wheat...They do not sow much barley here, because they do not reckon the profits very great. Wheat is so plentiful that they make malt of it.*

The midpoint of the eighteenth century finds the Upper Hudson and Albany County growing in both prosperity and population based largely on the expansion of the wheat farming and the exporting economy. The Dutch culture remained strong and, to a large degree, autonomous. Changes were coming, however, that would see the introduction of a stronger British presence that at first was welcome but soon became the cause of division.

1750 TO THE REVOLUTION

Great change came to the Upper Hudson and Albany County in the 1750s. The French and Indian War brought an influx of intercolonial and British troops as well as the instability of being at risk of conquest. William Johnson was the owner of a huge and growing estate, as well as a major figure in the defense of provincial New York from invasion from the north by New France. He was the First Baronet of New York and British

Sir William Johnson was instrumental in the eighteenth-century development of the Upper Hudson Valley's brewing industry. It was Johnson who opened trade routes between native groups and settlers in northern New York and the Mohawk Valley with Albany and Manhattan. These trade routes allowed for the movement of grain—especially wheat that was coveted for brewing—from the fertile growing areas of the state. *Albany Institute of History and Art.*

superintendent of Indian affairs. His center of power was to the western side of Albany County, where his alliance with the Mohawk Nation gave him formidable power.

During the early years of the war, Johnson kept records of his personal expenditures in the defense of the empire, and it is clear that he used beer as a means to build confidence and reward loyalty. On June 4, 1755, for example, he obtained two barrels of beer from Hendrik Fry for the Mohawks at Conajoharee to drink a toast the king's birthday. He purchased six more barrels on June 28, 1755, as part of preparations for the meeting with the nations of the Iroquois to establish their loyalty for the upcoming battles against New France.

A few years later, Johnson directed an Iroquois warrior to stand guard at the property of the brewer Barent Vrooman of Schoharie. Other familiar names show up in his documents. A Lieutenant Vrooman, as well as one named Visher, was named in his accounts in 1759. These may have been members of the immediate brewing families or, perhaps more likely, cousins by that time removed from the original trade that established the families who were moving across the west of Albany County to fill in the frontier. The overall effect of Johnson's war records indicates a mixed community—Dutch, British and Mohawks joining to stand against the common French enemy. It would not last.

New York, unlike other colonies, had detachments of regular British soldiers located within the colony throughout the entire royal period. They were stationed there due to the colony's strategic location south of New France in the Champlain and Hudson Valleys as well as the presence of significant Iroquois military strength in the area. In the late 1750s, during the French and Indian War, scurvy broke out at Oswego and Fort Stanwix. In response to the danger, General Jeffery Amherst, commander of the British forces, gave instructions to provide for spruce beer throughout the army. Following the fall of Ticonderoga, Amherst noted in his diary that "our brewery things at last got up...[and] will save several lives." The process for making spruce beer is set out in the 1759 orderly book from Amherst's expedition north up Lake Champlain:

> *Spruce Beer will be Brewed for the Health and Conveniency of the Troops, which will be served at prime Cost; 5 Quarts of Mollasses will be put into every Barrel of Spruce Beer; each Gallon cost nearly 3 Coppers...Each Regiment to send a Man acquainted with Brewing, or that is best capable of assisting the Brewers, to the Brewery to-morrow Morning at 6 o'clock, at the Rivulet on the Left of Montgomerys...One Serjt. of the Regulars and one of the Provencials to super-intend the Brewery, who will be paid is 6d per Day. Spruce Beer will be deliverd to the Regiments on Thursday Evening or Friday morning.*

The taste for spruce beer was not limited to the regular troops. Colonel John Bradstreet led the daring final raid on Fort Frontenac, defeating the French and separating New France in two in 1758. He served as deputy quartermaster general at Albany and is recorded in a letter as having given a gift of a cask of spruce beer earlier in the decade.

After the war was won and New France conquered in 1760, William Johnson continued to import beer into his western Albany County estate, but the records indicate that his choices were not local. By this time, he was buying Taunton ale from England as well as beer by the New York City brewer Lispenard. His change in preferences may reflect his further increased wealth, as he was also seeking out port wine and New Jersey cider from his southern supplier, the merchants Hugh & Alexander Wallace. Their invoice to Johnson dated November 3, 1772, shows the extent to which he would go to pour himself and his guests the range of beers he desired:

6/-/- for 3 Barrl Strong Beer at 40/
4/10/- for 3 Barrl. Ale @ 30/
1/7/- for 6 Barrels at 4/6
7/-/- for 10 Barrels Newark Syder at 14/
0/3/- for Carting ale to the Sloop

Note that Johnson is buying three grades of beer in addition to satisfying his taste for Taunton ale. Tauton ale appears regularly in notices placed by merchants in New York City newspapers of the 1750s and 1760s. Before the events that led to the Revolution, goods from the old country were prized and sought out. Taunton ale appears in these notices next to other imported temptations like Irish linens and old Gloucester cheese. One notice in particular indicates how Taunton ale set a standard as the shopkeeper advises that he has, lately imported, a limited supply of English beer "not inferior to Taunton ale." As a strong barley ale, it would have set itself apart from the indigenous hoppy wheat beers made by the Dutch brewers.

The peak of British culture in the third quarter of the 1700s announced through these merchants' notices foreshadowed the division of Johnson's frontier lands from Albany County as the new Tryon County in 1772. Around the same time, British institutions like the Masonic Lodge were being established in the Upper Hudson. At Albany's Union Lodge in 1765, future enemies like the owner of the Kings Arms tavern, Tory Richard Cartwright, faced revolutionaries-to-be, including members of the Dutch brewing establishment with names like Gansevoort and Visscher. For now, the community remained peaceful despite the new British tone, but further change would soon come.

The end of the British era in the Upper Hudson came about in a tavern brawl in the heart of the city near the original palisade walls of the Dutch fort. Exactly twenty-one years to the day after similar celebrations of the Mohawks at Conajoharee (now the town of Canajoharie) were enlivened by the gift of William Johnson's barrels of beer, in the early hours of June 4, 1776, townspeople were awakened by the sound of gunfire from the Kings Arms inn at the corner of Beaver and Greene Streets. While not dividing perfectly on cultural lines, there was an evident tendency among established Dutch families toward independence. This can be seen in the membership of groups such as the Sons of Liberty and the Committee of Correspondence, Safety and Protection. On that night, their opponents, the loyal Tory leadership, had gathered with their supporters to celebrate the birthday of George III with songs, toasts and bumpers, as well as gunfire. Denounced by Albany's Revolutionaries as an indecent daring insult, the event broke any remaining tenuous balance within the community.

Consequences were swift. The owner of the Kings Arms inn, as well as his namesake son, Richard Cartwright Jr., avoided the immediate fate of the others, including the Mayor Abraham C. Cuyler and county clerk Stephen De Lancy, who were sent to Tory jail in Hartford, Connecticut. Though they kept their liberty, the Cartwrights lost their tavern, their other property and their livelihood before making their way north to Canada in exile, uncertain of the future. The Cartwrights were joined by many others as the loyal Tories of Albany and the Upper Hudson left their farms and homes to an uncertain future in Canada. In May 1776, a month before the celebrations in Albany, to the west, Sir John Johnson, the Second Baronet of New York, fled north after becoming aware of a force being sent to arrest him and his supporters. He immediately set about raising the King's Royal Regiment of New York in large part from his loyal farming neighbors, tenants and Mohawk allies.

After the first half of the 1770s, when New York exports of grain and flour to England continued to expand to an all-time peak, the war brought hardship to both sides in the Upper Hudson region. Crops were destroyed, trade was disrupted and any semblance of normal life was lost. Even the Dutch Reformed Church suffered a division due to the influence of Methodism and the Great Awakening movement. During the course of the war, the Tory forces, made up of a mix of loyal farmers and Iroquois warriors, kept the breadbasket to the north and west of Albany from Revolutionary control. After the war, they would settle to the north of the St. Lawrence River and Lake Ontario and continue the unique monarchist Tory culture that had developed in the Hudson Valley during the century from the 1670s to the 1770s as one of the founding communities of the future nation of Canada. And as soon as the crop was in, they also returned to brewing their beer.

THE REVOLUTION TO 1800

As with all wars, the years of the Revolutionary War were bad ones for crops and brewing. Even with the defeat of the British forces in 1777 at Saratoga, through the years of conflict, Albany faced the British to its north in Quebec; the British to its south beyond West Point, who were in possession of New York City; and the British to the west, burning farms of the Mohawk and Schoharie Valleys. The frontier was being put to the torch by the Tory raiders, in many cases the farms' former owners. In 1780, New York governor Clinton advised Washington that Schenectady had become the western limit of settlement in the state. While there was certainly some communication with the outside world for those of position with connections among the leadership of the opposing force, Albany faced isolation. The breweries of Albany that had been active for a century and a half largely fell silent.

The Revolutionary War, along with the destruction of the farms and depopulation of the region, left another legacy that caused the collapse of the agricultural and brewing economy in the 1780s. Poor harvests, the introduction of a pest called the Hessian fly—named after the hated mercenaries brought in by the British—simple overproduction and tired soil were responsible for a collapse in wheat production from which the area would not recover for decades. The historian Alan Taylor has described how, in the late 1780s, hunger was a constant misery in the central New York frontier lands, which were rapidly filling with farmers from New England. William Cooper, an important landowner in Otsego, stated in the spring of 1789 that there was "not one pound of salt meat nor a single biscuit" for the two hundred starving families around him.

In response, local independent farmers turned to greater grain crop diversification. In turn, the loss of surplus wheat from the former export-focused monoculture led to a shift in the form of beer being brewed in the Upper Hudson. The strong wheat ale enjoyed by Daniel Denton in the 1660s and witnessed by Peter Kalm in the mid-1700s would soon fade away due as much to the change in agricultural practices as to the loss of Dutch cultural autonomy.

In time, recovery from the war and reversal of the depopulation of the lands came. The years of failed harvests for both agriculture and brewing were done. The ambitious noticed. William D. Faulkner began his brewing career in New York City in the late 1760s. Faulkner initially partnered with New York City merchant Leonard Lipsenard—the son of Albany brewer Anthony Lipsenard—and then with Stephen Rapalje and Anthony Ten Eyck

The oft-forgotten campaign executed by British soldiers, Loyalists and allied Iroquois forces to ravage and burn settlements and farms in Mohawk and Schoharie Valleys culminated in the massacre at Cherry Valley—shown in this engraving titled *Incident in Cherry Valley—Fate of Jane Wells*, based off the painting by Alzono Chappel. The destruction of 1,200 farms on New York's frontier had adverse effects on the brewing industry in the Upper Hudson Valley for twenty years after the cessation of fighting. *Courtesy of the Library of Congress.*

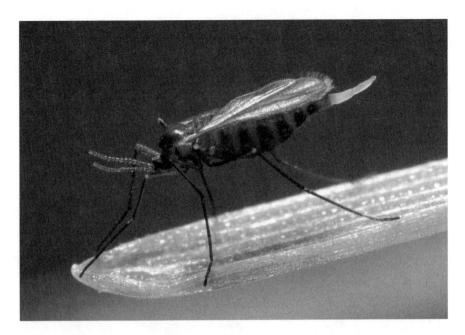

Mayetiola destructor—or, as it is more commonly known, the Hessian fly—was thought to have been brought to North America in the straw bedding of Hessian mercenary ships during the American Revolution. The introduction of this pest would wreak havoc on New York's grain crops late during the late eighteenth and early nineteenth centuries. *Photo by Scott Bauer, United States Department of Agriculture, Agricultural Research Service.*

to sell bottled ale and beer, but by 1771, he had opened his own brewery on Cow-foot Hill in what is now the modern-day Harlem neighborhood of Manhattan. A fire in his New York brewery brought about his relocation to Albany, and in 1790, Faulkner began renting a brewery in the city's northern neighborhood of Arbor Hill advertising ales, porter, bottled ales and spruce beer. By 1792, however, William Gibbs had announced that he would be occupying that brewery. The further career of Faulkner is not known.

In the 1790s, General Peter Gansevoort, hero of the Revolution, had assumed control of the family business. Gansevoort was the son of the merchant Harmen and grandson of the brewer Leendert Gansevoort. Peter operated the brewery until 1805, when it was finally torn down and replaced with the hotel Stanwix Hall. The Van Schaicks, like the Gansevoorts, had become one of the Upper Hudson's most prominent families, but the fate the Van Schaick Brewery is a bit of a mystery. Anthony van Schaick died in 1737, but there is no record of a brewery being passed to his children in his will. There was, however, a Sybrent van Schaick operating a brewery in

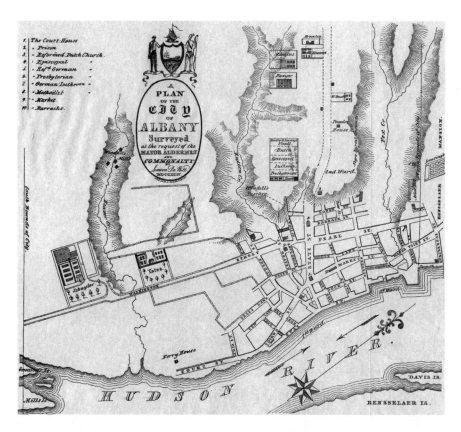

By the end of the eighteenth century, the city of Albany had doubled its land size, and its previous stockades had been removed. The city was also experiencing its first expansion west. Most importantly, however, was its ever-developing waterfront. The manipulation of the city's waterfront would eventually result in the building of the Albany Basin and the entrance to the Erie Canal in 1825. *Courtesy of the Albany Institute of History and Art.*

Albany during the 1790s. This Sybrent may have been the great-grandson of Anthony van Schaick.

Troy is a much younger community than its southern neighbor Albany. Settlements tied to the authority of the Van Rensselaers began to appear on the river north of Albany starting in the late 1600s. The development of what became the city of Troy didn't happen until much later. These small communities included Schaghticoke, an area settled by a diaspora of native peoples from eastern New York and New England, and the farm of Derick van der Heyden. Later, Abraham Lansing built his farm in the 1760s and eventually divided it into lots, forming what today is known as the village

BREWERY.

Peter Ganſevoort,

HAVING taken in partnerſhip JOSEPH LOCKWOOD, in the Brewing Buſineſs, they take this opportunity of acquainting their friends and the public, that in future that buſineſs will be carried on, under the firm of

GANSEVOORT *and* LOCKWOOD,

Who have for ſale, at their BREWERY, No. 23, MARKET-STREET, ALBANY,

Ale ;	Bottled Ale ;
Draft Porter ;	American Porter ;
Table Beer ;	London Do.

And a regular ſupply of freſh YEAST, for Bakers and private Families.

☞ J. LOCKWOOD, having for ſeveral years carried on the Brewing and Bottling buſineſs, in one of the principal towns in England, with conſiderable ſucceſs, he flatters himſelf they will be enabled to offer an article much ſuperior to that which has been generally manufactured in this country, and on this ground only they reſt their claim to public favor,

The higheſt price given for

BARLEY and EMPTY BOTTLES.

F O R   S A L E

An ad for the Gansevoort Brewery from the July 20, 1798 edition of the *Albany Gazette. Courtesy of NewsBank/Readex Database: New York State Historical Newspapers.*

of Lansingburgh. The city of Troy, due south of Lansingburg—originally known as Vanderhayden—was renamed and then incorporated in 1791 as a town. However, as a city, it was not chartered until 1816. It is most likely that a number of brew houses operated in the area in and around Troy prior to the 1790s. It is known that Colonel Steven Schuyler, brother of Revolutionary War general and New York State senator Philip Schuyler, was operating a small establishment, including a malt house, by that time.

Nothing better illustrates the return to normalcy in the last years of the century than an ad placed in 1798 by Peter Gansevoort and his new brewing partner, a new immigrant from England named Joseph Lockwood. The notice heralded the new era when it concluded with the promise that the highest prices were offered for barley and empty bottles. They were selling not only ale from their premises at 23 Market Street but also table beer and American and London porters in both bottle and cask. These would be new beers for a new nation facing forward into the new century.

Conclusion

The eighteenth century was clearly the most uncertain for those living in the Upper Hudson. The earliest years saw a continuation of the Dutch society founded the century before, but this was finally eroded as their interests were eclipsed by those of the British. In the middle third of the century, the British successfully adopted the earlier Dutch alliance with the Mohawk Nation, and together they defeated the great enemy to the north, New France. In the final decades of the century, the community was split by the Revolution and shattered by economic disaster and depopulation. Only in the last few years did the region recover and resettlement give some sense of the explosion of industrial progress to come. With these changes, a shift from wheat-based beer in traditional communities to barley-based ones came from brewers taking advantage of new opportunities from increased trade and modern transportation.

4

THE 1800s

Just as Albany and the Upper Hudson Valley entered the new century still recovering from the economic collapse that was left after the Revolutionary War, it began to cope with the mad rush of expansion west spurred on by new Jeffersonian ideals of personal liberty and entitlement. Where, before the war, the settlements to the west of Albany were under the control of large landholders like William Johnson and operated as something of a command economy, new settlers in the 1790s and into the 1800s were creating a population boom. New counties were carved out one after the other from what had once been the large expanse of Albany County.

By 1813, Genesee County alone had six breweries, two more than Albany. Albany, however, produced 297,000 gallons of beer annually, while Genesee brewed only 7,000. In fact, no other county other than New York itself comes within half the brewing capacity of Albany, according to Horatio Spafford's *Gazetteer of the State of New York* published in that year. With the rush westward to populate the emptying Iroquois lands toward Lake Erie and up toward the St. Lawrence frontier comes not so much expansion of brewing as a boom in small-scale rotgut whiskey distilling. Jefferson County, founded in only 1805, had just two breweries but sixteen distilleries. Distilling required far less stability and infrastructure than beer and met the needs of the sharp edge of a nation in motion.

THE STORY EDWARD A. LE BRETON

As the Upper Hudson recovered and grew in strength, new names appeared in the community, including among the brewers. The life of one brewer deserves a deeper discussion to illustrate the changes in mobility that the new era offered the ambitious. It is also worth reviewing because he may have changed one aspect of brewing in the Upper Hudson forever.

A humble little ad for bottled beer was placed in the *Albany Register* on May 5, 1803. The notice was from twenty-seven-year-old Edward A. Le Breton—gentleman, businessman and brewer. Le Breton was born in England in 1775. While his story is not known between that time and 1803, it is clear that at some point he partnered with Thomas Morgan to open Le Breton & Co., a brewery on Pearl Street in Albany.

Two years after the small notice appeared, another was placed in the March 22, 1805 edition of the *New York Morning Chronicle*—a Manhattan-based newspaper—that exalted Le Breton & Co.'s "Fine Albany Ale." As far as has been identified, the notice in the *Morning Chronicle* is the oldest record of Albany ale made by a specific brewer. There is a reasonable argument to be made that Le Breton, in fact, may have coined the phrase "Albany Ale," as a good number of ads for Le Breton's Albany Ale begin appearing in New York City and Albany's newspapers after 1805.

Capturing the slogan that would guide the path of Upper Hudson brewing for most for the nineteenth century, however, was not enough for Edward A. Le Breton and his brewery. Beer and ale adulteration claims were as common as horses in the nineteenth century, and it looks like Le Breton & Co. was no exception. In February 1807, the brewery issued an affidavit in both Manhattan and Albany newspapers that was witnessed by Sebastian (Visscher) Vesscher, master in chancery of the city of Albany, swearing that during the "mixing and finning of their ale, [they were accused of using] unwholesome and even poisonous materials, which report he, this deponent saith, is absolutely false, and without foundation."

Le Breton also offered the fantastic sum of $200 as reward for information leading to the libelist—big bucks back in 1807. Adding insult to injury for Mr. Le Breton, a New York brewer named Robert Barnes ran his own ad the following month in the same newspaper capitalizing on the sullied good name of Le Breton & Co. Mr. Barnes assured the public of his own amber ale's purity. In fact, he goes as far as to offer his product up for chemical analysis. How could the marketplace not trust him or not distrust those who would not offer up their own test results?

LE BRETON & CO.

FINE ALBANY ALE.—The public are informed, that they may now be supplied with the best quality of this Ale, by applying immediately on board the sloop Eagle, Albany Bason, or at Mr. Williams's 59 John street.   March 22   tt*

This ad, which appeared in the March 22, 1805 edition of the *New York Morning Chronicle*, is the earliest reference to Albany ale as associated with a named brewer or brewery—that of Edward Le Breton. *Courtesy of NewsBank/Readex Database: New York State Historical Newspapers.*

All of this seems to have had an effect on LeBreton's brewing fortunes, and it appears that the now thirty-two-year-old Le Breton began to have issues with his finances. By 1808, what appear to be insolvency ads, stating the need for "all persons indebted to Le Breton & Co." to make "immediate payment," had begun running in both Albany and New York papers. These ads are followed by a plethora of ads stating the consensual divorce of Le Breton from Le Breton & Co. Le Breton dissolved his partnership with Thomas Morgan but retained some ownership of the brewery. These ads run from 1809 through 1812. It is also during this period that Le Breton's wife died and he left Albany for Manhattan. Still, he had his backers. An article in the New York–based *Colombian* newspaper on December 21, 1811, vouches for the quality of Le Breton's beers—"Le Breton's Ale and Porter merit this encomium; and justice requires us to say, that their superiority and excellence have been admired and extolled by gentleman of the first taste and respectability"—and his reputation: "He has followed the business for a number of years in Albany; and his intelligence, experience and judgment, cannot be disputed." The article also mentions Le Breton's recent move: "Mr. Le Breton has lately moved into this city for the purpose of establishing a brewery."

Establish a brewery he did. Almost two years later, Le Breton announced the opening of his brewery near Spring Street in the Bowery of lower Manhattan in the January 28, 1813 edition of the *New York Gazette & General Advisor*. He acknowledged and thanked his loyal customers during his time in Albany and offered the same quality in his beer now being made in New York. He offered single ale at $5.00 per barrel, double ale at $7.50 per barrel and porter at $10.00 per barrel—notice, however, that none of his beers are referred to as "Albany Ale." Times seem to be good for Le Breton from this point on; nothing appears about him, or his brewery, until an article written by "A Country Brewer" pops up in the January 22, 1818 issue of the *New York Evening Post*. The author states:

> *There has been, for some years past, a meritorious competition existing among brewers, particularly of this city, in attempting to produce an article that would take best with the public, and be equal, if not superior (if possible) to the malt liquor produced in England. This laudable, (and advantageous competition to the public) commenced with the celebrated "Albany ale" brewed by a Mr. Le Breton, some years ago.*

Perhaps oddly, it appears that Mr. Le Breton moved again, leaving New York City, between the time that article was written and 1822. A short article from the *Albany Argus* on May 17, 1822, mentions a stop made by the forty-seven-year old Le Breton in Albany, en route to New York City with a cargo of ale. The article explains that many central New York towns were being supplied with Pennsylvanian beer, but the imminent opening of the Erie Canal might change that. Mr. Le Breton saw an opportunity in the market and opened a brewery in the Finger Lakes region near Geneva New York. Le Breton's time in Geneva was also short-lived. Seven years after establishing himself in Central New York, he moved west again, leaving for Michigan. In 1829, Le Breton established himself with the Detroit Brewery and began to make improvements to that facility. Shortly thereafter, in October 1830, the *Albany Argus* printed his obituary, taken from the *North Western Journal*. Edward A. Le Breton was dead at the age of fifty-five.

Le Breton's story spotlights the origins of Albany ale. The history of brewing families like Gansevoort, Taylor and Boyd has been shadowed over time, but there's still a record out there—beery dinosaur footprints, if you will. But how many smaller brewers, like Le Breton, have been all but erased from the collective conscience? Le Breton's story shows the nature of brewing in the early nineteenth century—the fickle nature of the beer consumer, the backstabbing of the industry and how quickly the facts were forgotten. But perhaps there's an aspect of Le Breton's involvement with Albany ale that is even more important. Le Breton may not have been the first brewer to make Albany ale, but he does—at this point—seem to be the first one who referred to the beer by that name. Perhaps, since the product was being brought into Manhattan, the name was simply a way to differentiate it from beer being made in New York. Or perhaps the way the words trip off the tongue made for a compelling brand. In any event, if he was the first to use it, he certainly was not the last.

FOUR OTHER BREWERS OF ALBANY ALE

One thing is clear from the record: Le Breton was not alone. In the early decades of the 1800s, as the repopulation of upstate New York took place, there was an influx of Scottish- and English-born immigrants whose numbers included many brewers opening small breweries in and around Albany. Soon, many more advertisements for a beer specified as Albany ale begin to appear, including in more distant towns and neighboring states. In these notices published in other cities, it is rare to see the beer named by brewery. What is advertised is simply described as "Albany Ale" or, less often, "Albany Strong Beer."

An extraordinary example of the latter was published in the *Kingston Gazette* on April 27, 1816. Kingston is an upper Canadian town that was settled by Loyalist Tory citizens of Albany like the Cartwrights and Sir John Johnson after the end of the Revolutionary War in 1783. Given the notice was placed just one year after the conclusion of the War of 1812—itself largely a repetition of the same issues and tensions—it is quite extraordinary that the beer held such attraction despite the obvious animosities between the communities. Perhaps there were still ties of personal allegiance and even taste preferences. Among these early Upper Hudson brewers of what was being called Albany ale were William Gill, William Gibbs, Joseph Ketchum, Jacob Cole and William Wake as well as the partnership of McLeish & Birrell. Most of these brewers opened and closed their breweries in quick succession, but a few breweries from the early decades of the 1800s had more lasting success.

One of these breweries just managed to reach into three separate centuries even if it lasted only 120 years. In 1796, Scottish-born James Boyd established a brewery at Arch and Green Streets that is considered to be the first modern brewery in the city of Albany. James's son Robert took over brewery operations in 1800. Partnering with Hawtorne McCulloch, Robert changed the brewery's name to Boyd & McCulloch. Robert bought out his partner in 1828 and ran the brewery with his son John as Boyd & Son. In 1852, Robert retired, and then his second son, David, joined the firm, which operated as Boyd Bros. & Co. until 1857. From that point, the brewery was run by the firm of Coolidge, Pratt & Co. Although the Boyd family no longer operated the brewery, they did retain an interest in it. In 1863, it was renamed the Albany Brewing Co., and it operated under variations of that name until closing in 1916, called at that time Consumer's Albany Brewing Co.

UPPER HUDSON VALLEY BEER

ALBANY ALE.—A constant supply o
Albany Ale, made by Gowey & Co. fo
sale by the barrel, by
JOHN CRANEY, Agent,
corner of Goveneur & Cherry-sts.
m 14-tf   at $5 per bbl.

By the second decade of the nineteenth century, Albany ale was regularly advertised in both Albany and New York City newspapers. *Courtesy of NewsBank/Readex Database: New York State Historical Newspapers.*

m xr.   100 Front-st.

SHIP Stores.—150 casks old London Brown Stout, 3 years in bottle
400 casks single, double and triple Albany Ale,
for home consumption and exportation
100 boxes good Bordeaux Claret
20 do. red and white Vin De Grave
Philadelphia, Albany and Connecticut Porter,
in hhds. and bbls. and some 12 months in bottle—
For sale at the market prices, and on accommo-
dating time.—Apply to   WILLIAM CROW.
m 20   93 Water-st.

rJ   Rice and Cotton.

A famous Hudson Valley name is connected to a brewery that existed in the first two-thirds of the nineteenth century. At nearly the same time that James Boyd was opening his brewery, James Vassar opened a brewery ninety miles south in Poughkeepsie, New York. James Vassar and his eldest son, John Guy, ran the brewery until 1811, when it was destroyed by fire, in which John Guy was killed. Opposed to becoming a brewer before the fire, James's younger son Matthew opened his own small brewery at the age of eighteen in order to save the family's fortunes. James's working notes, in the form of a daybook from 1808 to 1811, have been preserved. It shows a local marketplace of farmers delivering small lots of grain by the bushel and hops by the pound to the brewery. The same log shows small beer or ale by the gallon or barrel, as well as bottles of porter, being taken away by a small number of regular buyers, likely nearby tavern owners.

Over the next two decades, the younger Vassar's ale was in high demand. By the 1830s, Matthew Vassar had the largest brewery in the country, exporting his ale to many cities along the East Coast. Although Vassar did not live in Albany, evidence shows that, by the 1830s, his double ale was very similar to the ale being brewed in Albany—and might, in fact, have been sold as Albany ale. By the 1860s, Vassar had amassed so much wealth that he endowed an all-female college in Poughkeepsie now known as Vassar College. The M. Vassar & Co. Brewery operated until just before the turn of the twentieth century.

Another new brewery gave brewing a name that would live on for over two centuries. Scottish-born Robert Dunlop opened his brewery in Albany in 1806. By 1810, it was located on the eastside of North Market Street (now Broadway), just above Quackenbush Street, and was one of the largest in the city, brewing three thousand barrels a year. By the 1820s, Dunlop had amassed quite a fortune. He owned grain and plaster mills near Syracuse and malt houses in West Troy and Albany in addition to his brewery. It was at this time that Dunlop hired fellow Scot Peter Ballantine as his brewer. In 1834, Ballantine bought Dunlop's Market Street brewery. Dunlop went on to concentrate on his milling and malting business, eventually partnering with his son-in-law, Thomas McCredie. Dunlop's son, Archibald, oversaw the family brewing business in Albany, operating a new brewery on Quay Street. Upon his father's death, Archibald also partnered with Thomas McCredie in a brewery at the West Troy malt house location between 1852 and 1856.

Peter Ballantine continued to grow the old Dunlop Brewery, which he renamed Peter Ballantine & Co. He moved the brewery from Market Street to Lansing Street in the late 1830s and then finally out of Albany, relocating to Newark, New Jersey, in 1840. The brewery Ballantine opened in Newark evolved into P. Ballantine & Sons, one of the largest, privately held corporations in the United States by the mid-twentieth century.

The Burt Brewery was another successful brewery of the early nineteenth century. Uriah "Uri" Burt opened his brewery in 1819 at Colonie and Montgomery Streets. The brewery grew during the 1820s, eventually encompassing the whole block between Montgomery, Lumber, Centre and

Colonie Streets. The building's square, monolithic appearance became a landmark in the north end of the city. By the 1860s, the brewer was producing fifty thousand barrels per year. Tragedy struck in March 1865, however, when Burt's son and then head of the brewery, Charles, was killed when a large stone fell from the brewery roof.

These breweries of the Upper Hudson in the first decades of the new century illustrate the changes society was experiencing. Where Dutch culture had changed slowly for a century and a half, progress was moving the region rapidly forward in the early 1800s. The beers being brewed were barley based, were being brewed by larger and larger operations and were beginning to be intended for customers at a distance.

ALBANY AND THE ERIE CANAL

Despite now being thought of as an inland state capital filled with bureaucrats, Albany at this time was far more the industrial seaport, more in line with the wharfs of New York and Philadelphia. The city's waterfront—or what would become known as the Albany Basin—and the entrance to the canal was a manufacturing and mercantile core with businesses and manufacturing plants lining the riverfront. The river itself was crowded with schooners, skiffs and packet, steam- and canal boats. When the nearly mile-long Albany Basin pier was built in 1825, it had moorings for one thousand canal and fifty steamboats, not to mention the innumerable docks and slips built for private businesses.

By 1840, Albany was already 226 years old as a settlement and 152 years old as a chartered city. It was the sixth-oldest and longest continuously chartered city in the country. At the Revolutionary War's end in 1783, the city of Albany's population was between 2,000 and 2,500. In 1790, it was just over 3,000 people. By 1810, it had become the tenth-largest city in the United States with over 10,000 residents and would stay in the top ten until 1860. As of 1840, the Albany-Schenectady-Troy triangle was the sixth-largest metropolitan area in the country with almost 60,000 people. Although Albany never rivaled New York, Boston or Philadelphia in size, it was quite a bit bigger than most other cities and towns in the United States at that time.

Albany's position on the Hudson River, and in turn the location of the canal, was not happenstance, and its advantageous location becomes a repetitive theme throughout its history. Looking back to the very first

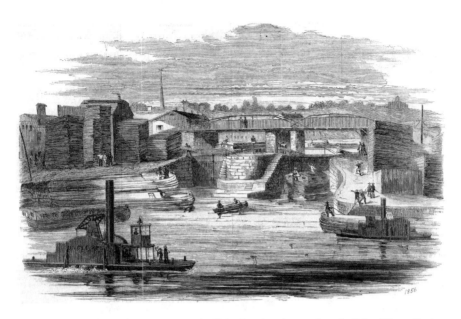

This illustration shows the entrance to the Erie Canal at the north end of the Albany Basin. *Courtesy of the New York State Museum.*

experiences of Europeans on the river, Albany's prime location was obvious. Robert Juet noted in his 1609 diary that Henry Hudson and his expedition explored the river "to nearly 43° of north latitude, where it became so narrow and of so little depth that he found it necessary to return." Latitude forty-three degrees north is about thirty miles north of Albany. The river at Albany was perfect for maneuvering a ship—just over one thousand feet between the west and east banks. The river near Albany and Troy was anywhere between twelve and forty feet deep, but farther north, it shallowed to an unnavigable seven feet. When the Dutch returned to the area in 1614, they knew not to venture farther up the river, instead settling near modern-day Albany—first at Fort Nassau and then relocating ten years later to Fort Orange.

In addition to the river's having a good width and depth near Albany, there's another phenomenon that Hudson may have noticed: it flows in both directions, north and south. What Hudson probably didn't know was that the Hudson River is actually the Hudson Tidal Estuary, which flows through the Hudson Fjord, formed during the last North American glaciation. The Hudson is a partially enclosed coastal waterway, with a number of rivers and tributaries flowing into it. It is also brackish, a mixture of salt and fresh water. All that makes it an estuary rather than a river.

As an estuary, and therefore technically a coastal body, it is affected by the tides. Approaching high tide, the river flows north. At low tide, it ebbs seaward. The tidal effect can be seen, and more importantly felt, four times (two high and two low tides) a day as far north as Troy—150 miles from the mouth of the Hudson. That means masted ships sailing up or down the Hudson didn't necessarily need wind for propulsion when traveling along the river—if of course, they were traveling at the right time of day. It also meant that steam-powered craft didn't need to expend as much fuel under those same conditions. A passenger on board Robert Fulton's steamboat the *North River* on its 1807 inaugural run from New York to Albany and back again noted the tides in a letter to the English press: "The next morning we left Albany with several passengers on the return to New York, the tide in favor, but a head-wind. We left Albany at twenty-five minutes past nine A.M. and arrived at Claremont in nine hours precisely, which gave us five miles an hour. The current, on returning, was stronger than when going up."

Coincidentally, 1807 was also when the Erie Canal was first seriously proposed. However, it is no coincidence that the canal's terminus was in Albany. The valleys formed by the Hudson and Mohawk Rivers are the only passages in the Appalachian chain north of Alabama, essentially making an unobstructed corridor from the port of New York to the Ohio Valley. Cutting the canal from Albany inland to Schenectady gave access to the waterway without causing congestion on the Hudson and at the mouth of the Mohawk. A canal boat could enter the canal through the Albany Basin and travel parallel to the Hudson north through West Troy (which gave access to Troy on the east bank of the Hudson) before eventually arcing at Cohoes along the curve of the Mohawk toward Schenectady to follow the natural cut made by the tributary valley. From Schenectady, the canal snaked along its big brother, the Mohawk, to Rome, New York, before continuing west on its own. In 1823, the Champlain Canal opened, connecting Lake Champlain, the Champlain Valley and Montreal to the Hudson River.

Albany was front and center in a perfect storm for shipping and trade by 1830. Albany controlled the flow of goods and products east–west and north–south for the entire Northeast. It was a fully established, large city with an infrastructure to support industry. It had access to an easily navigable, large coastal river and boasted a large inland seaport. And the canal? Well the canal changed everything, didn't it? Access to the Adirondack forests and mountains jump-started the area's lumber and iron industries, and clay deposits along the Hudson blossomed into a huge brickmaking industry. These bricks became renowned for their durability and were shipped across

This circa 1840s label (most likely affixed to a barrel rather a bottle) was from Uri Burt & Co. Early on, Burt took advantage of the city's distribution network. After leaving Albany and traveling south on the Hudson, portions of his cargo could be offloaded at the Port of New York for sale (and further exportation) at his Manhattan and Brooklyn depots. Additional shipments were sent to Springfield—via the Hudson to the Long Island Sound and Connecticut River—or to Boston. *Courtesy of Bob Kay, bobkaybeerlabels.com.*

the country via the canal. Let's not forget the beer. Grain from the Ohio Valley and western New York—along with hops—could be brought to Albany along the canal in about a week. Within a month, ale made from those raw ingredients could be on board steamboats heading to the Port of New York to be shipped across the globe.

While the canal was a blessing, it was also a curse. It was the first gateway to the West. Although it brought goods and products to the city, it took people away. Villages in the West became cities in the West, and those cities became competitors—Buffalo, Cincinnati, Chicago, St. Louis, Kansas City and San Francisco. As efficient as the canal was, innovation and demand was faster. As the western cities grew, a new form of transportation exploded—the railroad. On May 10, 1869—a mere forty-four years after the opening of Erie Canal—the first transcontinental railroad connected San Francisco to the East Coast rail lines at Council Bluffs, Iowa. Travel from Albany to Buffalo on the canal took a week to ten days. By rail, travelers and goods could make it to California—six times farther—in nearly half the time. Albany would never recover.

1820 to 1840

The Rise of Large Ale Brewers

The fifty-year time span between 1820 and 1870 would see the rise to dominance of the large, industrial ale breweries in the city of Albany. In the first part of that era, we see the expansion of the breweries of Albany as they take advantage of new transportation links and their own established resources, as well as embrace new technologies. Capitalizing on the opening of New York's new water highway—the Erie Canal—in 1825 and the city's access to the Port of New York via the Hudson River, the breweries of Albany would exploit western New York's grain- and hops-growing capability. The ease with which raw materials could be brought into the city, as well as the monopoly of distribution the canal and river afforded, allowed Albany to launch its namesake ale into the spotlight. By the mid-nineteenth century, Albany was shipping its beer as far as its sailing ships could reach.

Looking back from the bicentennial year of the Dongan Charter in 1886, at the outset of the 1820s, Albany was described as having four main breweries: Boyd & McCulloch with a brewing capacity of 3,000 barrels, Robert Dunlop at 3,000 barrels, Fidler & Co. at 1,500 barrels and Henry Birrel with 1,000 barrels. Albany beer was being sold in Connecticut. Albany brewers were starting to apply scientific advances in their brewing as part of greater agricultural advancements. In the April 27, 1827 edition of the *American Farmer*, a letter was published about a well being bored to supply the Boyd & McCulloch Brewery that had some surprising characteristics:

> *About the middle of May last, Messrs. Boyd and M'Cullock, commenced boring for water, in their extensive Brewery, in the south part of this city. When they had proceeded 70 or 80 feet, they came to a slate rock, similar to that found at Saratoga and Ballston, and they have now reached the depth*

of 500 feet, and are still in this rock. When the auger had penetrated 130 feet, a current of hydrogen gas (inflammable air) was found to issue at the surface, which readily ignited and burnt on applying a flame to the orifice But what is most remarkable, within a few days the water has risen within two feet of the surface, and on tasting it, it is found very similar to that of the Congress Spring, at Saratoga…and possessed, I think, a stronger saline flavour. It has been so far analyzed as to ascertain that it is of about the same specific gravity as the Saratoga water, and holds in combination, soda, magnesia and lime.

In the same letter, the state of brewing in the region was described. The author states that there was more ale brewed in Albany than in any other town on the continent. He notes that there were five main breweries, one of which was "aided by a twenty horse steam power" and was capable of turning out 240 barrels of beer a day. He states that Albany ale had earned a high reputation and "the immense quantity furnished at these establishments has a ready sale in the domestic and foreign market." Malting in Albany had expanded greatly in the previous two years, moving from 220,000 to 300,000 bushels a year. Barley and hops were described as "important staples" that contributed essentially to the agricultural profits of the region.

In May 1832, a brewer from Upper Canada named William Halliwell passed through Albany on his way from the capital at York before heading south to catch a ship to England. He rushed to visit two of the more prominent breweries in the city and noted what he saw in his roughly drafted diary:

I then went in search of Mesrs Fidlers & Taylors Brewery[.] I was luckey [sic] as to find Mr Fidler and he directed the brewer to show me through the Brewey[.] And relly [sic] I was surprised to find it so extensive[. T]hey mash 380 Bushels and brew sevn [sic] times per weeke[. T]hey mash by a mashine drove [sic] by a Steam Engine[.] The brewer told me that that they brewed 20000 Barrels of beer and that they had 3000 on hand which I think is an exaggeration from the fiu [sic] I saw[.] I think the brewery and malt house covers [sic] an acre of ground[.] They hav[e] three kilns and a brick floor[.] I also went to see Boyds Brewery which is verey large[. H]e mashes by steam and brews 5000 Barrels[.] His Engine I could carrey on my back verey [sic] well[. H]e has about 3000 bushels of malt in hand which he has covered with malt…To prevent the air from slacking it he has three kilns But think that two would dry all the malt that the floore can make.

Clearly, the brewers of Upper Canada were still well aware of the Albany reputation as Halliwell sought out the opportunity to learn what he could in a very brief stop before catching a ship to New York. He had a critical eye, noting both the scale of each operation as well as its use of new technologies.

Whatever Albany ale was in the 1830s, it was remembered with fondness later. In an 1899 article in the *New York Times* entitled "Kicked 90 Years Ago Just the Same as Now," a ninety-six-year-old New Yorker named Charles H. Haswell, who was still employed as a municipal engineer, was interviewed about his life and the city's old days. Talking about his youth in the 1820s and '30s, he noted that there were now fewer saloons and that drinks were bought in grocery stores. He said, "Albany ale was the beverage then that lager beer is today, and a mighty good drink it was. Mead and spruce beer took the place of soda water."

The life cycle of three breweries founded on three separate locations illustrate the expansion of Albany brewing during the middle half of the 1800s. One dynasty, founded by the Amsdell family, illustrates a height of the development of brewing in Albany during this time. In the 1830s, William Amsdell operated a small brewery on Rose Street while also employed as the head brewer at John Taylor's brewery on Green Street. He left his employment with Taylor and moved his brewery—along with his two sons, George and Theodore as apprentices—to what is now Guilderland, New York. He operated on the Great Western Turnpike now known as U.S. Route 20 until 1856. Two years earlier, having purchased the White Malt House and Brewery in 1854 at Lancaster, Jay and Dove Streets in Albany, the elder of the two brothers, George, opened his own brewery. Younger Theodore would join his brother in partnership three years later, thus establishing the Amsdell Brothers Brewery. Throughout the 1860s and '70s, the brothers grew their business into one of the most dominant ale breweries on the East Coast due to the popularity of their Albany XX Ale. Eventually, the brewery produced 100,000 barrels annually. In the early 1890s, Theodore left the partnership to buy into the Dobler Brewing Co. George renamed the original brewery after himself, George I. Amsdell Brewery, and then changed the name to Amsdell Brewing & Malting Company.

Another brewery followed a different path, even if it did not stay in the hands of a single family during this period. In 1832, Scottish immigrant Andrew Kirk opened a modest brewery in North Albany on Broadway, just north of Van Woert Street. Partnered with John Outwin for the first two years, Kirk separated from his partner in 1835 and eventually outfitted the brewery for steam power, making it the first in the city to take advantage of that technology. Kirk would continue to operate the brewery on Upper Broadway until his death in 1857. The building sat idle for a few years after Kirk's death, until Patrick Kearney and James McQuade began operating at the site in 1860. In 1867, the property was sold to Wilson & Co. and operated until John Smyth and James Walker purchased it in 1870. The Smyth & Walker partnership would continue until Smyth's retirement in 1877. Walker continued to operate the brewery until his death in 1879. In 1882, the Fort Orange Brewing Company operated at the site until 1889. While the brewery changed hands a number of times, William Kirk, son of Andrew, would continue to operate his father's malt house, just south of the main brewery, well into the late 1880s. Today, one of the original buildings from the brewery now is home to Stout, an Irish-themed pub.

Working as a brewer for the small firm of Howard & Ryckman in the 1830s, John McKnight opened his own brewery on Broadway, just above Orange Street in 1840. Later, McKnight relocated to the corner of Canal (now Sheridan Avenue) and Hawk Streets, as well as built a malt house on the next block over on Hawk and Orange Streets. In 1860, McKnight's son, William, took over operations, and by the mid-1860s, the brewery was known as J. McKnight's Son until 1875. The building was not used as a brewery again. It would, however, be bought by maltster Thomas McCredie.

Emigrating from Scotland in the late 1830s, McCredie, on the advice of his fellow Scot Peter Ballantine, began working in the malt houses around Albany, eventually rising to the position of superintendent at Robert Dunlop's facility in West Troy. McCredie left Albany briefly for a malting position in Philadelphia. Upon returning, he partnered with his former boss, Robert Dunlop, who also happened to now be his father-in-law. He bought Dunlop's Clinton Avenue malt house after Dunlop's death and began an arrangement with John McKnight for exclusive rights to operate McKnight's malt house. After McKnight's death, McCredie purchased that property and eventually the brewery property as well. By 1886, McCredie owned four large malt houses in and around Albany and a fifth in Boston, Massachusetts, making him one of the leading maltsters in not only Albany but also the entire United States.

The generational transition of prominent brewing families continued. In 1834, a map was surveyed of the lots in the fifth ward of the city of Albany belonging to Peter Gansevoort Jr. This Gansevoort was the son of the last of the brewing Gansevoorts, General Peter Gansevoort, who concluded his career early in the military administration of the new Republic. The map is now in the collection of the New York Public Library and shows the family holding substantial lands between Market Street and the shore of the basin for four blocks along the north side of Spencer Street. Before becoming a judge and trustee of the New York State bank—and in addition to being the uncle of the author Herman Melville—the younger Peter Gansevoort was also a member of both the state assembly and senate in the 1830s. He was sitting as a senator during the inquiry that led to the 1835 report of a select committee of the New York State Senate into the state of brewing in the Hudson Valley and New York City. The reason for the inquiry is described in the introduction to the report:

> *It was charged that the ale, beer and porter manufactured in this State was adulterated by the use of various drugs; some of which were represented to be of a noxious and unwholesome quality. Those charges were made, so far as the committee were* [sic] *advised, in a paper published in the city of Albany, and in order to investigate their truth, the committee caused a letter to be addressed to the conductor of that journal, requesting such information upon the subject as it might be in his power to communicate. The Senate is already aware, that he refused to comply with that request, unless the committee should be cloathed* [sic] *with power to send for witnesses, and to take their examination…When the Senate refused to grant such power, the committee were* [sic] *desirous of proceeding no farther in the investigation. But the manufacturers expressed so strong a desire of having an opportunity to exculpate themselves, from the charges, that the committee deemed it strict justice to afford them that opportunity.*

Taking advantage of the opportunity to publically dispel recent rumors of unsavory brewing and malting practices, a who's who of the brewers of the Upper Hudson Valley filed answers under oath to a specific set questions proclaiming the purity and sanctity of their trade. Along with soon famous brewers like Taylor, Vassar and Ballantine, the senate committee received evidence from the following extensive list of brewers:

> *E. Parmelee & Co. and J. Dougrey & Co, Lansingburgh; Nash, Burt & Co. and J. and N. Wallace, Troy; Fidler & Ryckman and their*

workmen, Andrew Kirk, Peter Ballantine and his workmen, White, Barker & Co., John Taylor and his head brewer, and Robert Boyd, Albany; George Robinson, Hudson; Hazard & Gardiner, Catskill; M. Vassar & Co., Poughkeepsie; Law, Beveridge & Co., Newburgh; D.R. Tittle, Dobbs' Ferry; John Johnson, Brooklyn; R.C. Wortendyke and his son, C.&S. Milbank, Wm. McMurtee & Co., Sagebury & Sherwood, W.B.&A. Miles, David Jones, J.M. Mounsey & Co. and workmen, S. Samer, Henry Buncc and his foreman, Thomas Kelley, Wm. Kinch and his foreman, and George Retching and his foreman, New-York; Thomas Reed & Son, Troy.

The report is an impressive record of the state of brewing of the day. In their submissions to the committee, the brewers give fairly detailed descriptions of their operations, including the proportions of malt and hops used per barrel. Below is an excerpt of the testimony given by Thomas Read of Read & Sons of Troy:

Say from 3 to 3½ bushels of malt to the barrel, and from 2½ to 5 pounds of hops to a barrel, and about four quarts of fine salt to 60 or 70 barrels; say in our pale, we put about two or three pints of honey to the barrel, we think makes the pale ale finer, and is rather an improvement; but we use none in brown beer; the malt is the chief material used, and the article which chiefly communicates the different tastes, qualities and colour to the beer and ale; and the different shades are chiefly owing to the manner in which the malt is dried on the kiln, and in some measure to the colour of the hop. When we make pale ale, we always select the palest malt and the palest bales of hops. We use no water, but pure, clean water, formerly from a spring, and at present from the city water-works.

While the senate testimony gives a good idea of Read's ingredients and the quantity of those ingredients, the process by which it was made is laid out in more detail in the second of two surviving brewing log books of Matthew Vassar from the mid-1830s, now in the collection of Vassar College. Although Vassar was not, strictly speaking, an Upper Hudson brewer, his records show that the ingredients used to make his pale "Double Ales" in the 1830s were very similar to those used to make the ales brewed by Read. Both beers contained very similar ingredients: pale malt, honey, salt and similar amounts of hops.

UPPER HUDSON VALLEY BEER

The beer being brewed in the Upper Hudson Valley during the early part of nineteenth-century seems to be closely related to those brewed in Britain, though not necessarily by those of the major brewing areas of London and Burton-upon-Trent. Those area's X and XX ales were more highly attenuated and more heavily hopped. The sweeter and more mildly hopped Upper Hudson Valley ale of the early 1830s, like Albany ale, bore more resemblance to those ales brewed in the English countryside and were not unlike those made at the end of the eighteenth century.

One particular characteristic mentioned by a number of the brewers in their testimony was that they used such a heavy amount of hops that the pale ale could be discolored if the palest hops were not used. Interestingly, Lancelot Fidler of Fidler & Ryckman admitted to also adding ginger and coriander seed on the occasional special order. In the years that followed, the scale of brewing would have likely seen such special touches pass.

1840 to 1870

John Taylor and Large Scale Exports

By the 1840s, Albany ale was recognized as one of the standard forms of American beer. It was referenced in scientific studies, such as one edition of the inelegantly titled *A Treatise on Food and Diet: With Observations on the Dietetical Regimen Suited for Disordered States of the Digestive Organs...*by English pharmacologist Jonathan Pereira:

> *According to Brande, London Ale contains 6½ per cent, of alcohol, or 13 per cent, of proof spirit; porter, 4¼ per cent, alcohol, or 8½ per cent, proof spirit. Small beer, 1¼ per cent, alcohol, 2½ per cent, proof spirit. According to Dr. L.C. Beck, Albany Ale in barrels contains 7.38 per cent, alcohol, or 14.76 per cent, proof spirit, while that in bottles has 10.67 per cent, alcohol, or 21.34 per cent, proof spirit.*

A lengthy discussion on the medical effects of strong ale follows, in which Periera concludes, "In health such drinks are not only useless but in general injurious," reflecting a new scientific perspective that would, over the coming decades, politically replace traditional assumptions about beer and health though the temperance movement.

The market for Albany ale was extending its reach through the 1840s. In 1846, two hundred barrels were advertised for sale in New Orleans, and just one year after Texas joined the Union, a Mr. Forbes was offering it for sale in Port Lavaca, Texas, on the Gulf Coast. In 1847, it is listed as being sold by the hogshead in the Newfoundland newspaper, the *Public Ledger*, on October 12, 1847. In 1849, the *Merchants' Magazine and Commercial Review* made mention of it as follows:

> *The business of malting and brewing is carried on to a great extent in Albany, and employs a large amount of capital. Six breweries and malt-houses of the largest dimensions were erected in this city the past year, and the whole number of such establishments is about twenty. The demand for malt liquors is daily increasing in the United States, and Albany ale and beer are found not only in every city in the Union, but likewise in the West India islands, in South America, and in California. The annual product of the breweries of Albany is estimated at 80,000 barrels of beer and ale. Capital invested, $500,000. Bushels of barley purchased annually, 500,000.*

In the whole history of Albany ale, no figure stood so high and fell so far from the public's imagination than the brewer John Taylor. In 1849, his brewery would have been one of the largest and likely the one with the farthest export reach. His brewing facility stretched along the riverfront for hundreds of feet at its peak and had custom-built dockage for loading his beers for export around the eastern coast and beyond. Taylor was born in England around 1790 and immigrated to the United States with his family when he was a child, arriving first in Brooklyn and settling in Albany a few years later.

By the time Taylor was seventeen, the industrious youth had started his own his own candle-making business with backing from his father. Fire was a constant threat to the candle-making industry. Taylor's factory was not immune as fires broke out in his factory at least four times. But he was not deterred. A contract with the U.S. Army in 1813 provided enough capital for him to switch his business from candle making to brewing. By 1819, Taylor had married Mary Richmond and, within a few years, had accumulated enough money to open his first brewery at 70 South Pearl Street in Albany with his brother-in-law Lancelot Fidler (who later went by Howard) as partner.

The year 1825 brought the opening of the Erie Canal, which connected Lake Erie with the Hudson River. A savvy businessman,

This portrait of John Taylor was painted in the mid-1830s, when the brewer was about forty-five years old. By this time, Taylor had established himself as one of the most successful brewers in the city. *Courtesy of Dennis Holzman Antiques.*

Taylor saw an opportunity to exploit New York's new water highway. He could import grain and hops from the western part of the state, make his beer in Albany and then ship it south to the Port of New York via the Hudson. In 1833, Taylor bought out his brother-in-law's half of the brewery and relocated his production to a larger facility on Green Street just beyond where the walls of the original Dutch fort had stood two hundred years before.

In the mid-1830s, however, his success had made him a target. A former wine merchant turned prohibitionist, Edward C. Delavan, publicly accused Taylor of using stagnant and contaminated water to produce his beer. Taylor then sued Delavan for libel in 1835 in a case that made headlines across the country. It was one of the first widely publicized pro-temperance legal battles involving beer.

Calls for statewide or national temperance of alcohol began in the United States well before the time of John Taylor, but during the first part of the nineteenth century, New York was becoming a hotbed for the antidrink stance. It was being fueled by the absolutist ideals and social activism of the Second Great Awakening as well as the nativist, often anti-ethnic views of many political parties during the antebellum period.

By the late 1820s, however, politics and infighting had fractured the early temperance movement, and its progress had stalled. The movement had split, with moderates allowing some responsible drinking on one side and total prohibitionists like the Connecticut preacher Lyman Beecher, who advocated against the use of any and all liquor, on the other. It would be the latter group, led by the Edward Cornealius Delavan, that that would set its crosshairs on the brewers of Albany.

Delavan, a one-time wine merchant in New York City, benefited from the success of the Erie Canal and profited so greatly in the real estate market that, by 1827, he had amassed enough of a fortune to retire—at the age of thirty-four—to the outskirts of Albany. It was at this time that the young Mister Delavan denounced his previous boozy employment and took up the cause of temperance. Within two years, he and his like-minded cohorts had founded the New York Temperance Society. Delavan evangelized the virtues of temperance to the wealthiest of Albany society, asking them to lead by example by discarding their expensive, imported wines. His zealotry, however, hit a fever pitch when he mounted a campaign against eucharistic wine in the mid-1830s, a position seen as tenuous, even by his own society members. But that didn't stop Delavan.

The number of breweries in Albany made the city's brewers an easy target for Delavan. In the 1830s, he began an all-out war on beer in Albany. He publicly denounced many of the city's breweries—including the maltster John G. White—but in a February 12, 1835 article in the *Albany Evening Journal*, he took it one step further. Delavan claimed that John Taylor was drawing water with which to malt from a pond contaminated by the rotting corpses of animals dumped there by slaughterhouses and glue factories as well as from a stream that passed through the cemetery of the city's almshouse. Although the claims against Taylor were the worst, Delavan targeted a number of brewers, and $300,000 worth of libel damages—from seven other of the city's brewers—would be brought against him. Ultimately, though, only John Taylor's suit was prosecuted.

Arguably the city's most well-known brewer and the one with the most to lose, Taylor filed his a libel suit against the prohibitionist in 1835. The case would not go to trial until five years later. The trial itself lasted six days with some seventy witnesses testifying on both sides. Try as they might to discredit Delavan, Mr. Taylor's lawyers fell short in that task—most likely since Taylor had indeed been using putrid water. Delavan proved this without a shadow of a doubt and was acquitted, and Taylor was ordered to pay cost. You would think that Delavan's damning revelations would have collapsed the Albany brewing industry, but as George Rogers Howell so eloquently notes in his 1886 publication, *Bicentennial History of the County of Albany*: "Higher ground was taken; and more aggressive and stringent methods advocated." All people involved seemed to have washed their hands of the whole affair. The city's brewing industry didn't collapse; in fact, it boomed, and Taylor continued brewing and became infinitely wealthy—he was later even elected mayor!

But the effects would be felt. Eventually. You see, Edward Delavan was sneaky—or, more to the point, a skillful propagandist. His intended goal was not to destroy the brewing industry in a single upstate city but rather to seed the prohibitionist mantra across the country. What better way to do that than to involve himself in a legal case that garnered national headlines and saw him acquitted. The mighty John Taylor played right into Edward Delavan's hand. Albany's biggest brewer was a patsy in the very best sense of the word—and he appears to have been never the wiser. Delavan continued to use guerrilla techniques to spread the word of prohibition into the 1860s. The Taylor case would be the first teetotaling salvo against beer, and it was lauded among prohibitionist into the twentieth century. *Taylor v. Delavan* was one of the first widespread, mainstream disseminations of the antidrink message, a message that would gain so much momentum in the eighty years after the trial that it would result in a thirteen-year ban on alcohol in the United States.

Taylor's life was not fully absorbed with his brewing and certainly not with his fight with Delavan. Throughout Taylor's adult life, he kept a logbook. This book is now held by the Manuscripts and Special Collections Department of the New York State Library. This log recorded much of the brewer's business and personal life from the 1820s until the late 1850s, much of it having little to do with brewing. In it, he kept detailed records of stock holdings; a tally of his steamboats, eleven total at the time of the count; a list of books in his library; photographs of friends and family; and numerous sketches, including one of a possible waterline for his Green Street brewery. One unusual entry is a poem written by Taylor and presented to a Mrs. Wallace, along with a half barrel of his X ale. It reads thusly:

> *We are not old, but will be so*
> *If spared to run times steady flow*
> *Age creeps apace, not can we stay*
> *Its onward course, a single day.*

> *Where* [illegible] *this, on life's decay,*
> *Some tonick might be brought to pray*
> *But what! Ah here, it doth perplex*
> *maderia, whisky, or Taylor's X*

> *This last they say is rightly taken*
> *well settled down, but never shaken.*
> *Will cheer us up, keep wrinkles off,*
> *Give us strength, and cure a cough.*

> *Some even say, will muse inspire,*
> *fire the mind with Poetic fire,*
> *Make us forget our troubles here*
> *Cause us to think of naught but cheer*

> *If half what's said is only true*
> *of Taylor's X, then will not you*
> *receive a cask of foaming ale*
> *will finish this a rhyming tale*

> *With compliments*

> *J. Taylor*

Taylor's Arch Street and Broadway brewery consisted of a six-story main building, a five-story malt house (a second was built later), several secondary buildings encompassing two full blocks, a grain elevator and its own slipway into the Hudson. Taylor traveled to England in 1850, visiting a number of that country's breweries—most notably from the Lion Brewery in London's South Bank. He brought back with him many ideas and concepts that would eventually develop into the technology for his new facility. *Courtesy of the Albany Institute of History & Art.*

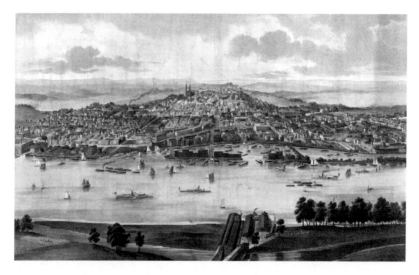

This lithograph by John W. Hill shows the city of Albany as it appeared in the mid-1850s. The Albany Basin is clearly visible, running nearly the full length of the city's waterfront. Aside from the Basin, Taylor brewery can be seen at the far left of the image, as well as the Boyd & Brothers brewery behind that. *Library of Congress.*

By 1851, Taylor had built a new brewery at Broadway and Arch Streets in Albany. It was the largest brewery in the country, capable of producing 200,000 barrels of beer a year. Taylor began producing a flagship double-strength XX ale, which he dubbed Imperial Albany XX Ale. As demand for this double-strength ale grew, so did the number of breweries in the city—twenty-four by the mid-1860s—many of them producing some variation of Albany ale. By the start of the Civil War, Taylor & Sons had also become one of the most technologically advanced breweries in the country: it used pressurized kettles capable of boiling up to 1,000 barrels of unfermented wort at any time.

In the 1850s, cargoes of Albany ale continued to be shipped from Newfoundland to as far as California. According to the *Daily Alta California*, the good ship *Citizen* out of New Bedford brought a mixed cargo from the East Coast to San Francisco that included Albany Ale, pickles by the barrel, butter by the firkin, China teas and building materials, along with whole prefabricated framed cottages. These were premium products for a new booming Pacific coast frontier.

And Albany's brewing industry itself was booming to meet the new demand. The January 4, 1854 edition of the *Brooklyn Eagle* stated that the Albany breweries were manufacturing more ale than the cities of New York, Philadelphia and Boston combined:

> *Albany ale is known over the whole continent. It is found as far north as Labrador and as far south as Chili [sic]. During the closing year nine breweries have turned out an aggregate of 233,000 barrels. The present price of ale is $5.50 per barrel. This makes the amount over a consumption of 600,000 barrels of hops, worth 35 cents per pound. The number of men employed about the breweries and malt houses is about 700; the number of horses 212.*

Albany brewers were establishing depots in other centers. Eccleston and Mise had agents at 177 Warren Street in New York City in 1854, a fact known because the fire that burned it down was reported in the *New York Times*. Around the same time, Uriah Burt had depots in Brooklyn, Boston and Springfield, Massachusetts.

Three other breweries come to the fore during this era: Quinn & Nolan Brewing Company; White, Barker & Pruyn; and C.H. Evans's brewery. Each had a continuing influence on Upper Hudson brewing history in a different way.

Irish-born James Quinn started his small ale brewery on North Ferry Street in North Albany in 1845, operating there for fifteen years. Returning home from the Civil War, James's son Terrance, took over brewery operations in 1865. Terrance's childhood friend Michael Nolan immigrated to Albany from Ireland in 1843. He left the Upper Hudson as a young man for the California gold rush. Returning to Albany in the 1860s, Nolan began working for the McKnight Brewery and soon reconnected with Quinn. By 1866, the two men had formed a partnership in what became Quinn & Nolan Brewery. Aside from brewing, Quinn also had an active political career. Serving first on Albany's Common Council, he was elected as a state senator in 1871 and was eventually elected to be a member of the U.S. House of Representatives in 1877. Throughout this time, he and Michael Nolan continued to run their brewery. The partnership lasted until Quinn's death in 1878 at the early age of forty-one. Nolan assumed sole ownership of the brewery.

From the late 1870s into the 1880s, Quinn & Nolan began to move away from Albany ale, advertising instead its "California Pale XX & XXX Ales," perhaps to capitalize on the fervor of westward expansion. By this point, Michael Nolan had himself become one of the richest and most influential men in the city of Albany. Following his partner's lead, he forged into the political world of Albany, first serving as the city's fire commissioner and then elected as mayor in 1878. Upon acquiring full control of Quinn & Nolan Brewing Company that same year, he saw the rise in the popularity of lager and completed his trifecta in 1878 by opening a dedicated lager-brewing facility, Beverwyck Brewery. Quinn & Nolan continued to operate separate from Beverwyck as the ale-producing arm of Nolan's brewing business for the next forty years.

The White brothers, William and John, took a different path to brewing wealth. They entered the brewing industry in 1823 with the opening of a small brewery and malt house between State Street and the Western Turnpike. In 1831, the brothers separated the brewery and the malting businesses with John controlling the malt house and William the brewery. The brewing operation was relocated to Dean Street. In 1832, William partnered with Samuel Pruyn and began operating the brewery as White & Co. Within two years, Charles Barker joined the firm and the brewery was named White, Barker & Co. But by the following year, 1835, William was no longer listed as a partner. It is unclear if this is to do with his death or simply that he left the partnership.

Now as Barker, Pruyn & Co., the firm continued for seven more years until being sold to William Eggleston in 1842. Samuel Pryun initiated the

Founded in 1845 by James Quinn, Quinn & Nolan would flourish under the leadership of James's son Terrance and his partner, Michael Nolan. A canal boat can be seen at the extreme left of the painting, rail lines are obvious to the left and the Hudson River is shown on the horizon—all nods to the brewery's ability to distribute far and wide. *Courtesy of the Albany Institute of History & Art.*

breakup of Barker, Pruyn & Co. by leaving to develop his family's lumber business. Along with Jeremiah and Daniel Finch, he eventually started the Glens Falls, New York paper company Finch, Pruyn & Company—today known as Finch Paper. Eggleston operated the brewery for the next twelve years with two separate partners—first Putnam and then Mix. The brewery finally closed in 1854, when William Eggleston left the beer-making business for the railroad industry.

Although the brewery closed, John White's malting business was a great success. Like John Taylor, White capitalized on the Erie Canal's ability to easily bring beer-making goods like barley and wheat to Albany from the western parts of New York State. Selling his malt house on Jay Street to George Amsdell, John partnered with his son Andrew in 1856 in the firm John G. White & Son and grew his business into one of the largest malting companies in the United States. By the mid-1880s the father and son held malt houses in Albany, Bath, New York City and Philadelphia. Combined, the four houses had the capacity to produce well over one million bushels of malt per year. John died in 1892. Andrew continued in the malting business until he retired in 1900.

Farther south, the merchant Robert Evans and his partner James Phipps purchased their brewery in Hudson New York in 1856. Its location along Mill Street had previously been home to a small brew house built in 1786 by Englishman Benjamin Faulklins. The new brewery and malt house had been in operation since 1836. In the late 1860s, Robert's son Cornealius H. Evans purchased his father's interest in the brewery. Cornealius would partner first with Phipps and then, after the elder partner's death, with Phipps's sons J.H. and James Gaul. By 1878, however, Cornealius bought out both men and became the sole owner of C.H. Evans & Co. Under Evans's leadership the brewery thrived, selling beer north and south along the Hudson River. The Evans Brewery operated until national Prohibition went into effect—but its name would return.

George Robinson had started an earlier brewery on North Second Street prior to purchasing Faulkner's brewery, which he sold to Benjamin Millard and Stephen Barnard. In 1864, Ezra Waterbury purchased Barnard's interest, eventually becoming the sole proprietor.

Albany lost a great businessman and citizen when John Taylor died in 1863. Two years later, a book—*Ale in Prose & Verse*— was commissioned by Taylor's sons Joseph and William to commemorate their father and his brewing empire. It was published in 1866. The book opens with an eleven-page poem titled "A Runlet of Ale," and the tome's authors, Barry Gray and John Savage, interweave the four-thousand-year history of brewing, a basic synopsis of beer making and various scientific and economic facts with flowery praise for the former mayor and brewing magnate. It is beery propaganda at its best. Although the book is a prime example of brewing hyperbole, it does offer a fantastic description of Taylor's mid-nineteenth-century facility. Gray and Savage note of Taylor's malt house and grainery:

> On the river front, connected with the main building, is a fire proof brick building, seven stories high, and seventy by forty feet in dimensions, which is used in storing the grain from which the malt is made. The majority of brewers throughout the country purchase their supplies of malt from those who manufacture it, as it requires a large capital to carry on both the malting and brewing business. Mr. Taylor, Senior, early saw the advantage to be gained, however, by combining the two branches, which would enable him to select the finest barley in the market, and personally superintend its malting.

R. W. EVANS & CO.,
BREWERS,
SUPERIOR PALE AND AMBER HUDSON
ALE,
Office, 51 Harrison St., cor. of West St.,
NEW YORK.

ROPT. W. EVANS, }
JAMES L. PHIPPS. }   WM. GAUL, Agent.

The brewery on Hill Street in Hudson, New York, was established in 1786 by Benjamin Faulkins; however, it was under the ownership of the Evans and Phipps families that it truly thrived. *Courtesy of the New York State Museum.*

They extol the engine and mash room: "Only steam could be successfully used as the motive power; hence we find in the engine room two double geared steam engines, of fifty horse power, constantly at work, running seven hundred feet of shafting." The authors also describe the brewery's brewing coppers: "There are two brewing coppers for boiling down the wort and hops; the larger one holds one thousand and the smaller six hundred barrels. By the aid of a threethrow gun metal pump the wort is discharged from the coppers to the coolers, at the rate of two hundred barrels per hour."

Along with these, Gray and Savage mention nearly every important aspect of John Taylor's brewery in exacting detail—from the water tank, cooling room and racking cellar to the coopering department, counting house and even the building's famous clock tower. The book is also adorned with a number of illustrations. Many of these engravings exalt Taylor and his famous ale, but others give a snapshot into the day-to-day world of a large, mid-nineteenth-century American brewery.

Within just a decade of Taylor's death all four of his sons also passed away. The brewery continued to operate for the rest of the century, but by 1900, it had been sold away from the family, though the brewery kept the Taylor name. Today, the riverfront site of his empire is the scene of a large U-Haul business and a highway interchange.

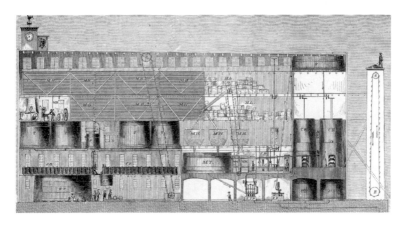

By the 1860s, Taylor & Sons was easily the largest brewery in the country. Taylor had adopted the latest brewing technology, including pressurized kettles, steam-powered pumps and a grain elevator. The brewery is said to have had a capacity of 200,000 barrels of ale per year. This cutaway of the brewery from the 1865 book *Ale in Prose & Verse* shows Taylor's expansive brew house operation. *Courtesy of the New York State Library, Manuscripts & Special Collections.*

Perhaps the most innovative technology in Taylor's brewery was its pontoons—an idea Taylor borrowed from the Lion Brewery. The pontoons were a conditioning system, similar to a Burton Union, by which ale was allowed a secondary fermentation in large, open-topped cedar vessels. Yeast built up on top of the beer, spilled out through the opening into a trough and was carried away, thereby refining the beer of excess yeast. Taylor's pontoon room had 365 pontoons, capable of holding just over 7 barrels each, meaning that about 2,600 barrels of ale could be conditioned at any given time. *Courtesy of the New York State Library, Manuscripts & Special Collections.*

Compared to ale breweries in Great Britain, especially London, Taylor & Sons was a small- to medium-sized operation. In the United States, however, it was unprecedented. This image of Taylor's racking cellar form *Ale in Prose & Verse* shows the size and scope of the brewery's capacity. *Courtesy of New York State Library, Manuscripts & Special Collections.*

Although some of Albany's ale breweries, like Taylor's, had become quite large during the period from 1820 to 1870, it is important to remember there were many smaller ale breweries operating in the city as well. Fidler (Howard) & Ryckman, D.B. Anderson, Sinclair & Walsh, John Artcher, Thomas Black and James Coyle are among those operating at the height of the Albany ale phenomenon. Spruce beer, once quite common in the colonial and postcolonial eras, was also becoming popular again with a number of breweries specializing in its production opening in Albany during the mid-nineteenth century. James Chester, Peter Mansfield and James Rockenstyre all made spruce beer during this period. The nostalgia did not last, and in any event, it was modern, progressive Albany ale that led the region's industrial brewing boom in the second third of the 1800s, not throwback spruce beer.

1870 TO 1880

The Beginning of the End for Albany Ale

The public record from the time casts an interesting perspective on the nature and effect of Albany ale. In a memoir of a Scots Presbyterian congregation written in 1850, a parishioner looks back in fondness to the previous decades when after a church meeting, a small picnic was held of cheese and crackers, ginger pop and Albany ale. Similarly, an 1845 article in the *United States Democratic Review* contains a cheery and likely completely overdone remembrance of the way politics ran in the good old days:

> *But touching that corner grocery once more. Know you, reader, that it is a short step from that same place to political preferment? There is a strange proximity between the end of a barrel and a seat in the Common Council…I maintain that your grocer, engaged all his time in dispensing so many of the luxuries and comforts of life, acquires a good feeling towards his fellows which fits him for public life. Besides his place is a favorite retreat for the hard-working business men, who in the evening assemble to discuss the occurrences of the day, and canvass freely the merits of men as well as measures. It was somewhat better arranged a few years ago, when New York was not quite so large. There was then a back room in which very staid and worthy citizens met to take a draught of "Taylors Albany ale" and play backgammon, and quietly settle who should be Alderman, and who President?…It was a great place for Bucktails and Federalists in times of yore. I verily believe that the Erie Canal had much aid from the pots of beer over which its construction was discussed.*

By the 1860s, the representations of Albany ale were no longer as positive. In an 1863 novel, *Hannah Thurston: An American Life* by Bayard Taylor, Albany ale appears in a sickbed scene. A character called Bute was recovering and no longer needed constant nursing; however, when he was left alone without his nurse, he sat "comfortably pillowed" and "consumed enormous quantities of chicken broth, and drank immoderately of Old Port and Albany Ale." The beer may have earned its reputation. In June 1865, an article appeared in a number of papers, including England's *Daily Telegraph* and Australia's *Sydney Morning Herald*, called "America in the Midst of War: Low Life in New York" in which Albany ale was seen described as sharing some pretty questionable company

The first "full-blooded" establishment we entered was many degrees noisier than the lager beer saloons. There was an atmosphere of roughness and rowdyism not to be mistaken. The same respectable and blue spectacled Germans were sawing away at the double bass or blowing lustily into brazen instruments in the orchestra; but little attention was paid to the music. There was much beer about, but it was not all lager. Philadelphia and Albany ale, and an especially nasty compound retailed in ginger beer bottles, and libellously called "Edinburgh ale," were plentiful; nor was a dreadful combination of turpentine and white rye whisky, falsely called "London Dock gin," wanting. This colourless poison is brewed from I know not what, unless from the most inferior rye, but it forms the basis of much hell-broth, sold indifferently as gin and whisky.

Another chronicler of that decade indicates that its reputation may have become tarnished:

As late as 1833, when the dome of Stanwix Hall was raised, the aged Dutchmen of the city compared it to the capacious brew kettle of old Harme Gansevoort, whose fume was fresh in their memories…Pleasantries at the expense of Albany Ale and its Brewers are not a recent thing. It was related by the old people sixty years ago of this wealthy Brewer, that when he wished to give a special flavor to a good brewing he would wash his old leathern breeches in it.

While gaining a somewhat dodgy reputation, Albany ale continued to be a beer of considerable strength. In a contemporary study of the late 1860s titled *Malt Liquors and Their Therapeutic Action* by Bradford S. Thompson, MD, of New York, it is shown in a table indicating the average quantity of alcohol in different common varieties of beer. Lager beer is shown as averaging 3.5

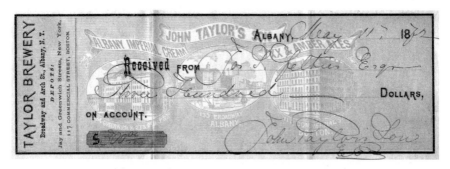

An 1872 receipt from the Taylor Brewery. *From the collection of Aaron Connor.*

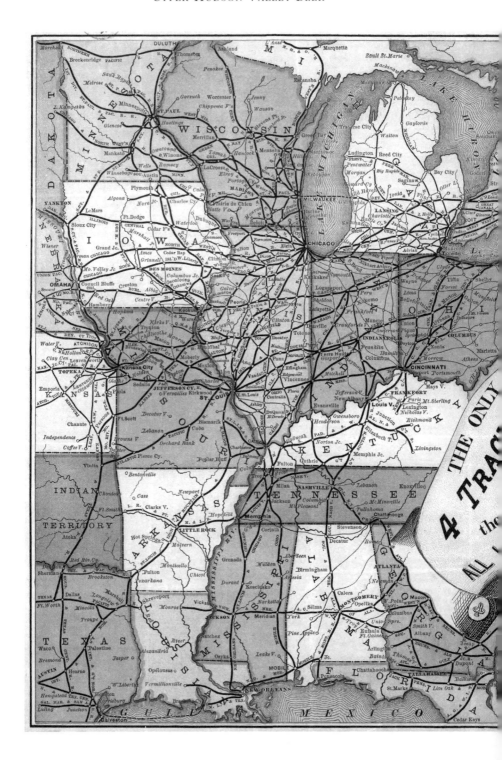

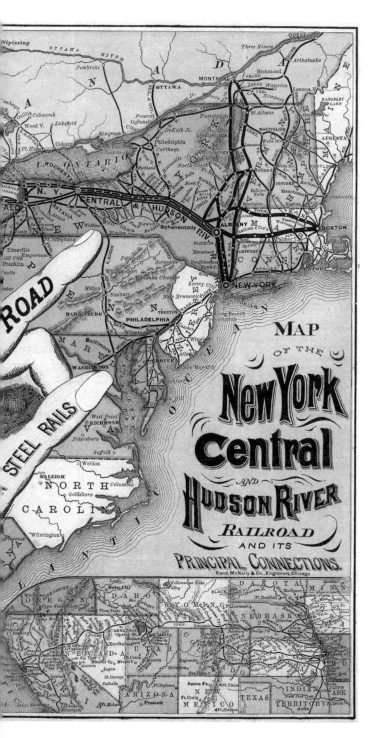

This map shows the extent to which the railroads had expanded by the 1870s. *Courtesy of the Library of Congress.*

percent and London porter 4.2 percent. Albany ale is stated to be on average an astounding 10.67 percent.

In the mid-1870s, the ascendency of temperance was a cultural norm. Albany ale could easily be identified with all that was wrong with alcohol. In a travelogue entitled *Our Next-door Neighbor: A Winter in Mexico*, the reputation of Albany ale is compared to a noxious Mexican drink called "pulque"—and is still found lacking:

> *It is the people's chief beverage. It tastes like sour and bad-smelling buttermilk, is white like that, but thin. They crowd around the cars with it, selling a pint measure for three cents. I tasted it, and was satisfied. It is only not so villainous a drink as lager, and London porter, and Bavarian beer, and French vinegar-wine, and Albany ale. It is hard to tell which of these is "stinkingest of the stinking kind." How abominable are the tastes which an appetite for strong drink creates! The nastiest things human beings take into their mouths are their favorite intoxicants.*

The late nineteenth century was a time for technological advancement in the American brewing industry, with many of the city's facilities switching to steam-powered coppers, pumps and mills. Bottling was also becoming more common. The expansion of the railroad during and after the Civil War greatly reduced the effectiveness of the Erie Canal as the Upper Hudson Valley's main importation and distribution channel and, with it, much of Albany's advantage. By the 1870s, rail lines crisscrossed a large portion of the United States, connecting the East Coast with the West. As a result, most towns and cities could easily get goods in and out of their localities, meaning breweries opening in large numbers in younger western cities like Rochester, Buffalo, Cleveland, St. Louis and Milwaukee were competing well beyond their local markets. Albany ale was no longer the export commodity it had once been. The beer produced in the Upper Hudson Valley by the mid-1880s on would be for local distribution only.

The period between 1870 and 1880 might be the most telling era of brewing in the Upper Hudson Valley during the nineteenth century. Aside from the rise of the railroads, Albany ale, the region's signature brew, had begun to tarnish, and demand for it was waning. The temperance movement had leeched onto its downfall, painting it as a totem of all that was wrong with fermented, alcoholic beverages. And by the mid-1870s, the first family of Albany ale, the Taylors, were all but gone. In many ways, the market and the brewing industry were moving on.

THE DEVELOPMENT OF LAGER

As we have seen, the story of Albany brewing in the 1800s is an ale story in that it is ale that built the brewing industry and ale that sustained it for the majority of its history. Lager is a small part of that history. Lager simply never gained a major foothold in the city and surrounding areas as it had elsewhere. Albany stayed very much an ale-brewing hub well past the point when lager had ascended to its beery height in the rest of the country.

Historically, ale brewing is far older than lager making, and its roots reach as far back as the early Middle Ages. Although popular elsewhere, today ale is usually associated with the United Kingdom, but that was not always the case. Because ale uses yeast, which best performs at warm temperatures (ideally between sixty-five and seventy degrees Fahrenheit), it was easily made in almost any environment—and was especially suited to the temperate spring and autumn seasons in Great Britain and northern Europe. Aside from its warm fermentation, top-fermenting ale yeast is also quite expeditious, and ale is often ready to drink within a few weeks of fermentation

Lager, on the other hand, needs both cold fermenting conditions (forty to fifty degrees Fahrenheit) and an additional cold environment for extended conditioning—up to six months in some cases—to achieve its crispness and clarity. The Bavarian Alps and their consistently chilly caves were perfect for this type of brewing. By the end of the eighteenth century, Great Britain's, and to some extent Belgium's, ale breweries had grown quite large. However, technologically and scientifically speaking, the lager brewers of Bavaria were still in the Middle Ages compared to these ale breweries—even as late as the early nineteenth century.

The first lager brewed in the United States was likely made in Philadelphia in the early 1840s, but it took a while for the cold-fermented trend to catch on, especially in the Upper Hudson Valley and Albany. It is not that lager wasn't being brought into the city or sold in the city. It was. There is just very little hard evidence of its being made there prior 1860. It did, however, get a fair bit of press. During the 1850s, Albany newspapers were rife with articles about "lager-bier" and the saloons in which it was sold, but the papers mostly reported on its appearance in other cities like Cincinnati and Baltimore and its differences from top-fermented ale. An article in the July 3, 1854 *Albany Journal* noted: "The frequency with which placards bearing this inscription meet the eye, the recency of its introduction into this city, and the cabalistic character of the words themselves may perhaps render a brief article upon this topic not uninteresting."

JOHN H. SUTLIFF,

Eastern New York Agent Phillip Best Brewing Co.'s Celebrated

MILWAUKEE LAGERS

Wholesale Dealer in MALT LIQUORS and MINERAL WATERS,

25 HUDSON AVE.,   **ALBANY, N. Y.**

ROSCHE & ROSHIRT,

(Successors to Hinckel's Brewing Co.)

SOLE BOTTLERS OF HINCKEL'S SPARKLING LAGER.

Manufacturers of SODA, SARSAPARILLA, GINGER ALE, &c.

48 CLINTON ST.,   **ALBANY, N. Y.**

E. C. ROSCHE.   Telephone Orders promptly attended to.   Telephone Call, 894 F.   F. ROSHIRT.

Although lager was not produced in great quantity in the Upper Hudson Valley, a good bit of it was imported. This advertisement for "Milwaukee Lagers" is from an 1889 Albany-Rensselaer City Directory. Phillip Best Brewing Co. would eventually become Milwaukee's Pabst Brewing Company. *Courtesy of the Albany Institute of History & Art.*

The article also mentions that "we know of but one lager brewery in New York" that sells lager. It is most likely that the article means New York City and not the state, but the scarcity of lager is suggested nonetheless. As far as Albany goes, it is known that Johann von Schlagenhauer was brewing as early as 1848, and Prussian-born Frederick Hinckel and Bavarian-born John Hedrick both opened breweries in Albany in 1852, making them the earliest central European immigrant–owned breweries in the city. What isn't known is if those breweries opened as ale breweries or lager breweries or possibly something else altogether. They may have been brewing Bavarian-style weiss bier or sckankbier. As the 1850s wore on, circumstantial references to lager brewing in Albany appear, but nothing notes a named brewery. In 1857, Templeton's—a furniture store on Albany's main drag, Broadway—advertised refrigerators for sale that are suitable for, as the ad expresses, "Grocers, Butchers, and Lager Beer purposes."

In 1852, Frederick Hinckel partnered with Johan Andreas Schinnerer to open Hinckel & Schinnerer, a small brewery between Warren Street (now Park Avenue) and Johnson Street (now Myrtle Avenue) at South Swan Street. The brewery sat on the north bank of the Beaverkill Creek in an area of the creek known as Buttermilk Falls, east of the Delaware Turnpike. The brewery itself was named the Cataract Brewery (*cataract* is an antiquated term denoting "a large or powerful waterfall"), although it was often simply referred to as Hinckle Brewery. As the popularity of lager grew during the 1870s, so did the brewery, as improvements were constantly being made to the facility. In 1880, a year before Hinckel's death, a five-story malt house and later an ice-making facility were added. In 1881, Hinckel's sons Charles and Frederick assumed control of the brewery. The brewery operated into the early twentieth century and was arguably the second-most successful brewery next to Beverwyck. Ultimately, it also closed due to national Prohibition. The Hinckel Brewery still stands today. It is the only full nineteenth-century brewery complex still standing in Albany. It was converted to apartments in the mid-1990s; however, its exterior is nearly as complete as it was in the early twentieth century.

Arriving in the United States in 1832 at the age of twenty-six, John Hedrick first immigrated to Baltimore and then moved to New York City. He finally settled in Albany. Like Frederick Hinckel, Hedrick also opened his brewery in 1852. Unlike Hinckel and his brewery located in the center of Albany's brewing industry, Hedrick's was so far away from the heart of the city that he might as well have been in California. The little brewery sat on a lot two miles west of the river on the corner of Bowery Street—now Central Avenue—and, what was essentially a cattle trail, Ontario Street. Although rural in 1852, this area known as West Albany would boom within a few years due in large part to the West Albany Rail Yard, built in the mid-1850s, and the relocation of the Albany cattle and stockyards to the area in 1860. Both industries brought jobs, and so also came an influx of Poles, Germans and Italians into the area over the next thirty years. As the Central Avenue corridor grew, so did Hedrick's brewery. Being so far from the river, and therefore without a consistent source of ice needed for cooling and refrigeration, the brewery dug its own ice pond. When Hedrick died in 1891, his son William stepped in as president and continued in that role until 1916, when the brewery was purchased by the Knickerbocker Brewing Corporation.

In 1865, Darius S. Wood built a small wooden structure for the purpose of brewing lager beer between Johnson Street and Elm Street at South Swan Street almost directly opposite the earlier established Hinkel brewery. That structure was bought three years later by John S. Dobler and, from that point on, became known as the Dobler Brewery. John grew the shack into a full-fledged, modern brewery, and it was passed to John's son August on John's death in 1885. It was bought by Theodore Amsdell and then by George Hawley seven years later in 1892.

Like the Dobler Brewery, the founding of T.D. Coleman & Bros dates to the late 1860s. In 1869, the Coleman brothers established their ale brewery at the corner of Chestnut and Lark Streets in what is now Albany's Center

FREDERICK DIETZ,
SUPERIOR
LAGER BIER,
McCarty Avenue, Corner South Pearl Street,
ALBANY, N. Y.

TELEPHONE 1223A.

Estate of JACOB KIRCHNER
Standard Lager Beer
BREWED STRICTLY FROM HOPS AND MALT ONLY.

BOTTLED BY KIRCHNER BROS.,

8 and 10 Sherman Street,   ALBANY, N. Y.

WM. SCHINDLER,
LAGER BEER BREWER,
RECTIFIER, AND WHOLESALE AND RETAIL
LIQUOR DEALER,
397 to 403 SOUTH PEARL STREET,
ALBANY, NEW YORK.

Frederick Dietz, Jacob Kirchner, William Schindler and Christian Rapp all opened lager breweries in Albany during the 1870s—with varying degrees of success. Generally small operations, most of these breweries produced well under fifty thousand barrels per year, even into the early twentieth century. The most successful of these German-founded operations—Dobler, Hinckle, Hedrick and Weber breweries—also made ale. *Courtesy of Christopher White, findingyourpast.blogspot.com.*

Square neighborhood—a block north of the much larger Amsdell brewery. James Kennah also operated an independent malt house directly next door to the Colemans. In 1882, he sold his property on Chestnut Street to the Colemans, allowing the brothers to expand their brewing and malting business. When the Colemans opened their brewery in the late 1860s, the Center Square area was not an overly developed part of the city. That would change within a few years. By the mid-1880s, it was becoming one of Albany's more fashionable neighborhoods. In 1896, Albany businessman John G. Myers bought the brewery, leveled the structures and between 1899 and 1900 built a series of fourteen row houses intended for young couples, known then as Bride's Row.

The Kirchner Brewing Company was established in the same year as Coleman's. Immigrating to the United States from central Europe, Jacob Kirchner opened his small lager brewery in 1869 near the juncture of Lark Street, Washington Avenue and the newly named Central Avenue. By 1877, the brewery had expanded and included frontage on Sherman Street, a street that ran behind the original location. Kirchner had also opened a small bottling facility a few blocks north on Spruce Street. Jacob, working with his son also named Jacob, operated the brewery until his death in 1882. From that point until 1905, the brewery operated in probate until being purchased by two local businessmen, Gustavus Sniper and Judson Bailey. Within a year, the two men would also purchase the Amsdell Brewing & Malting Company. They apparently reached too far and, unable to successfully operate the two businesses, had to close within ten years.

To be fair, the arc that lager brewing has taken thus far in Albany's brewing history isn't that far from what was happening in the rest of the county. By the 1870s, that had all changed. The 1870s saw the start of a significant German immigration to the United States, a trend that would continue over the next thirty years. The decade would also bring technological innovations and advancements in commercial refrigeration, both game changers in the world of lager. It should be noted that the America lager brewing was not simply a mimicking of central European lager brewing. Beer historian Ron Pattinson has noted that whereas European lager makers often employed the technique of decoction mashing (a method by which a portion of the mash is removed, boiled and returned to the main mash to raise its temperature), American brewers usually did not. Most American lager breweries simply performed a cooler primary and secondary fermentation and then left the beer to condition in cold storage—initially kept cold with ice and later with chemical refrigeration.

Because of the Erie Canal, Albany saw more people pass through it than stay. The city and its canal was the start of the journey, not the end. Albany also had a large, established ale-brewing industry—and ale breweries didn't need refrigeration to operate. This established ale industry was also hard to compete with. It was easier for wealthy German and central European brewers and businessmen to establish breweries in the growing West, in areas in which they had no serious competition and had growing, similar immigrant populations, cities like Buffalo, Cleveland, Chicago and St. Louis.

We see this in Albany's beer production numbers. In the 1850s and '60s, breweries like Amsdell and Albany Brewing Company had the capacity to produce 75,000 to 100,000 barrels of beer—and Taylor, the largest, even more. Hedrick and Hinckel were barely breaking the 1,000-barrel mark. By the late 1870s, a few small lager breweries had opened, such as those of Frederick Dietz, Jacob Kirchner and William Schinedler along with the larger Dobler Brewery. Hedrick and Hinckel were most certainly brewing lager at this point. Still, all the lager production numbers were dwarfed by the large ale breweries. Hinckel, by far the largest, was only capable of producing 30,000 to 40,000 barrels per year. The large ale breweries like Amsdell and Quinn & Nolan could more than double that output.

However, there would soon be a major exception to the ale trump card in Albany. In 1884, H.P. Phelps wrote in his *Albany Hand-Book: A Strangers' Guide and Residents' Manual* that for "many years Albany had been noted for its ale, but it was not until 1878 that it became equally famous for lager." That newly famous lager was from Beverwyck.

By 1880, Michael Nolan had become one of the richest and most influential men in the city of Albany, having acquired of Quinn & Nolan Brewing Company and been elected mayor of Albany. It was not by accident that he decided to take on both lager and ale brewing. Nolan was a modern industrialist who made his new lager-brewing facility, Beverwyck Brewery, the most up-to-date brewery in the city, boasting the most modern pumps, boilers and refrigerators available in the late 1870s.

Throughout the late nineteenth century, the twin breweries Beverwyck and Quinn & Nolan both expanded, ever increasing Nolan's wealth and power. In the early 1880s, following in his late partner's footsteps, Nolan, while still mayor, was also elected to the U.S House of Representatives and served from 1881 to 1883, returning to the city post for a short time after his stint in Congress. By the 1890s, the two breweries were easily the largest and most productive in the city, dominating the industry as Taylor's had a generation before. Beverwyck's 185-foot-tall chimney became a city

Michael Nolan, circa 1880s. *Courtesy of the Albany Institute of History & Art.*

landmark and, by the turn of the century, had been adorned with electric lights advertising "BEVERWYCK LAGER," literally becoming a beacon for the brewery.

Beer and graft went hand in hand—especially in Albany. Political influence ran deep in the capital city, and the ubiquity of beer made it an easy target for those with sticky fingers. One case involved a local saloon owner, Henry Dorr, Albany mayor John Boyd Thatcher and former mayor Michael Nolan. Dorr, a German immigrant and former liquor merchant, had opened the popular Cosmopolitan Saloon during the early 1880s on Broadway. His establishment, located between two of the city's most popular hotels, Stanwix Hall and the Delavan House, was the talk of the city, a saloon-goers dream. By 1886, the Cosmopolitan boasted a barbershop, shooting gallery, bowling alley and the "Best and Coolest Lager" in town. Dorr, having all these other amenities, decided he would also offer live music. What Dorr didn't realize is that he would be subject to obtaining an "amusement" permit from the city.

Dorr was arrested for offering music without the permit, saying he knew not of the ordnance, and was arrested a second time for violating the statute. The second time, he claimed that Mayor Thatcher had agreed to issue the permit, but unbeknownst to Dorr, the mayor had changed his mind. The saloonkeeper filed suit against the city, compelling the mayor to issue the permit, which only exasperated the issue. At this point, Michael Nolan stepped in.

In the late nineteenth century, Albany's Republican Party controlled the local government on both the city and county level. Nolan, as the former mayor just two years out of office and as a former member of the U.S House of Representatives, still held considerable sway in the back rooms of Albany City Hall. Nolan mediated the situation, appearing to act on behalf of Dorr. He negotiated with Thatcher to issue the permit if Dorr would pay a monthly $50 fee at a rate of $600 per year. In exchange for his service, Nolan would pressure Dorr to serve his Beverwyck beer instead of Hinckel's at the Cosmopolitan. Although a $600 permit was twice the rate of those for other establishments in the city, Dorr found he was unable to refuse the offer. On Monday July 11, 1887, he walked into Albany's City Hall and paid his $50.

The implication is that Nolan was behind the whole situation from the beginning. In fact, Albany's newspaper headlines at the time asked, "Who is the Mayor?" Ostensibly, it was Dorr's notoriety as the owner of the Cosmopolitan that garnered interest about the case in the first place, but it is most likely this was not a singular case. It is probable that Nolan used his political clout—during his tenure as mayor and after—to further the expansion of Beverwyck and his other concerns. This may be shocking today, but as we will see, the city's government forty years later would take corruption and coercion to a whole other level.

1880 TO 1900

Although the period from 1870 to the turn of the twentieth century would see the rise of lager in Albany, ale would continue to be the main

This image of John F. Wolf's tavern shows perfectly the duality of brewing in the Upper Hudson Valley during the late nineteenth and early twentieth centuries. The Hudson, New York establishment is receiving its shipment of ale from the city's hometown brewery, Evans, but also advertises a new alternative—Dobler Lager—from Albany. *Courtesy of Historic Hudson, Rowles Collection.*

product made by the majority of breweries in the city. Whereas in the majority of the country, lager was out-producing ale, in Albany, that was quite the opposite.

One example of new ale breweries entering the local market was the George F. Granger Brewery. The building owned by George Granger isn't so important to the history of Albany brewing as is the Granger family's connection to brewing in New York. Originally opened in 1874 on lower Central Avenue, the brewery was operated as three separate firms—McNamara & Mcloughlin, A.S. Long and Lemming & Paris—over the first six years of its existence. In 1880, however, the brewery was bought by George Granger, who moved its equipment to a new location at Broadway and Fourth Avenue.

The Granger family had ties to the brewing industry across the state. The Granger patriarch also owned a brewery in Hudson, New York, and operated as Granger & Gregg with his son William and partner Henry Gregg. Granger and Gregg purchased Ezra Waterbury's establishment on North

ADVERTISING DEPARTMENT. 487

GRANGER'S BREWERY.

GEORGE F. GRANGER, Proprietor.

Formerly with the Albany Brewing Company.

MANUFACTURER OF

CREAM ALES, PORTER

 AND

STOCK AND INDIA PALE ALES.

— ALSO —

GRANGER'S

FAMOUS BURTON ALES.

FOURTH AVENUE and CHURCH STREET,

ALBANY, N. Y.

Although this ad is for the Granger Brewery in Albany, the Grangers were one of the most prolific brewing families in New York State. *Courtesy of the Albany Institute of History & Art.*

This stained-glass, heraldic window is from the Reformed Protestant Dutch church in Beverwijck, erected in 1656. It shows the Jacobsen family crest. Rutger Jacobsen was an early brewer in Beverwijck, and this heraldry reflects that. Mash tubs and paddles are clearly visible adorning the crest. *Courtesy of Albany Institute of History & Art.*

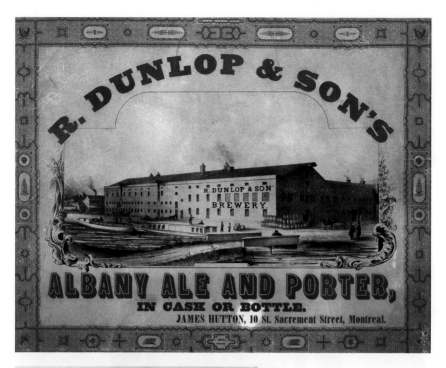

Above: Robert Dunlop was one of the most successful early nineteenth-century Albany brewers. This image dates to the 1840s and was used as an advertisement for Dunlop's agent in Montreal. *Courtesy of the Albany Institute of History & Art.*

Left: Although Albany ale was the most advertised product of the Albany brewing industry during the mid-nineteenth century, the city's breweries produced a broad range of ales. This lithograph for John McKnight's Son Brewery shows the variety of other beers made as well. *Courtesy of the Albany Institute of History & Art.*

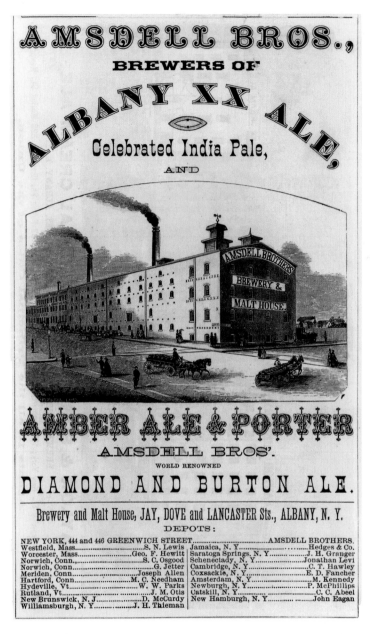

AMSDELL BROS.,

BREWERS OF

ALBANY XX ALE,

Celebrated India Pale,

AND

AMBER ALE & PORTER

AMSDELL BROS'.

WORLD RENOWNED

DIAMOND AND BURTON ALE.

Brewery and Malt House, JAY, DOVE and LANCASTER Sts., ALBANY, N. Y.

DEPOTS:

NEW YORK, 444 and 446 GREENWICH STREET	AMSDELL BROTHERS.		
Westfield, Mass.	S. N. Lewis	Jamaica, N. Y.	Hedges & Co.
Worcester, Mass.	Geo. F. Hewitt	Saratoga Springs, N. Y.	J. H. Granger
Norwich, Conn.,	S. C. Osgood	Schenectady, N. Y.	Jonathan Levi
Norwich, Conn.	G. Jetter	Cambridge, N. Y.	C. T. Hawley
Meriden, Conn.	Joseph Allen	Coxsackie, N. Y.	E. D. Fancher
Hartford, Conn.	M. C. Needham	Amsterdam, N. Y.	M. Kennedy
Hydeville, Vt.	W. W. Parks	Newburgh, N. Y.	P. McPhillips
Rutland, Vt.	J. M. Otis	Catskill, N. Y.	C. C. Abeel
New Brunswick, N. J.	D. McCurdy	New Hamburgh, N. Y.	John Eagan
Williamsburgh, N. Y.	J. H. Thieman		

By the 1860s, the phenomenon of Albany ale was at its zenith. Capitalizing on the earlier success of Taylor & Sons, George and Theodore Amsdell began advertising their version of Albany ale. It appears that, around this time, the generic term of Albany ale for any excellent beer made in Albany seems to have given way to something else. Amsdell Brothers and Taylor a few years earlier began to advertise "Albany ale" as a specific style of beer, listing it with other known types of beer. *Public domain image.*

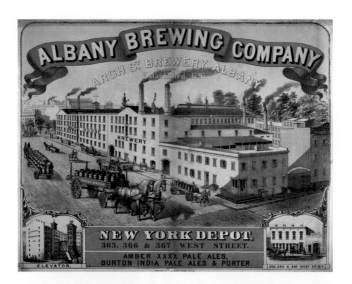

The Albany Brewing Company, originally the Boyd Brewery, had been exporting Albany ale to New York since the early nineteenth century and continued its strong exportation business well into the second half of the century. This image shows the brewery in Albany but also notes the address of the brewery's depot on Manhattan's Lower West Side. *Courtesy of the Albany Institute of History & Art.*

Although ale production dominated into the second half of the nineteenth century in the Upper Hudson Valley, the rapid expansion of the railroad during and after the Civil War retarded the effectiveness of the Erie Canal to transport goods. The Albany brewers began moving away from Albany ale as their apex product. Capitalizing on the furor of westward expansion in the 1870s, Quinn & Nolan Brewery began advertising its alternative to Albany ale— "California" pale ale. *Courtesy of the Albany Institute of History & Art.*

Samples of Albany and Troy breweries' beer bottles, circa 1880s and 1890s. *From the collection of Aaron Connor.*

By the turn of the century, Beverwyck Brewery had become the largest producer of lager in the Upper Hudson Valley. In 1906, the brewery's 185-foot-tall chimney was adorned with electric lights advertising "BEVERWYCK LAGER." *Courtesy of the Albany Institute of History & Art.*

For the majority of its history Albany was an ale-producing city, but by the first decade of the twentieth century, even it's traditionally ale-producing breweries began looking to lager. *From the collection of Aaron Connor.*

Left: Stollo was a malt-based but nearly nonalcoholic "Temperance Beverage" made by Stoll Brewery in Troy during Prohibition. *From the collection of Aaron Connor.*

Below: Half-gallon bottles of Stanton, Fitzgerald and Dobler beer, circa 1938. *From the collection of Aaron Connor.*

The Upper Hudson Valley had three breweries in operation for over 120 years. The brewery that became Evans Brewery in Hudson opened in 1786; James Boyd opened his brewery, which became the Albany Brewing Company, ten years later in 1796; and the brewery that became Stanton Brewery in Troy was opened by Abraham Nash in 1817. Only one of these three breweries survived Prohibition—Stanton. When Stanton finally closed its doors in 1950, it had been in operation for 133 years. *From the collection of Aaron Connor.*

Middle: A label and coaster from Quandt's Brewery in Troy, circa 1930s. *From the collection of Aaron Connor.*

Left: Tap handles from various Troy and Albany breweries, circa 1930s and '40s. *From the collection of Aaron Connor.*

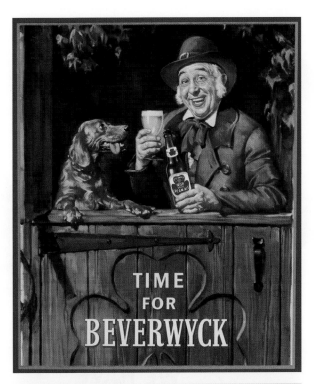

Lager had been Beverwyck's most popular pre-Prohibition brew, but its Irish Brand Cream Ale (perhaps a nod to the brewery's Irish roots) was by far its most popular post-repeal beer. The cream ale was so popular, in fact, that when Schaefer purchased the brewery in 1950 and discontinued the brew, public outcry was so loud it was reintroduced under the Schaefer name as Schaefer's Irish Brand Cream Ale. *Courtesy of the Albany Institute of History & Art, from the collection of Aaron Connor.*

Above: Bill Newman's brewery on Learned Street in Albany was a stone's throw away from a number of Albany's historic breweries, including the Schaefer Brewery complex on North Ferry Street, Andrew Kirks's brewery on Broadway and Peter Ballantine's brewery on Lansing Street. *Albany Institute of History & Art.*

Opposite, top: Schaefer, Hedrick and Dobler beer of the 1950s and 1960s. *From the collection of Aaron Connor.*

Opposite, bottom: Fitzgerald Brothers breweriana of the 1950s and 1960s. *From the collection of Aaron Connor.*

Top: This bottle of Newman's Saratoga Lager from 1993 was contract brewed by the now defunct Catamount Brewery in White River Junction, Vermont. Newman also contracted with Utica's F.X. Matt Brewery and Hibernia Brewery of Eau Claire, Wisconsin. *Courtesy of the New York State Museum.*

Left: The Big House Brewing Company was the first brewpub to open in Albany. Located on Sheridan Avenue, it opened its doors in 1996. The restaurant and brewery saw early success but, by 2000, began to falter. Expansion to a second location on Wolf Road in the Albany suburb of Colonie, New York, and a shift in focus from food and beer to a nightclub format, proved too unstable to sustain. By 2003, both locations were shuttered. *From the collection of Colleen Ryan and Eric Hoppel.*

Brown's Brewing Co.'s Pale Ale. *Photo by Craig Gravina.*

Left: C.H. Evans's Belgian Wit and Poor Soldier Porter. *Photo by Craig Gravina.*

Below: Keegan's Mother's Milk. *Photo by Craig Gravina.*

Top: Aside from its anchor beers—Kingfisher and Mendocino—Olde Saratoga brews its own line of Saratoga beers and has contract brewed for Keegan's, Southampton and City Steam, among others. *Photo by Craig Gravina.*

Left: Steadfast Sorghum Pale Ale. *Photo by Craig Gravina.*

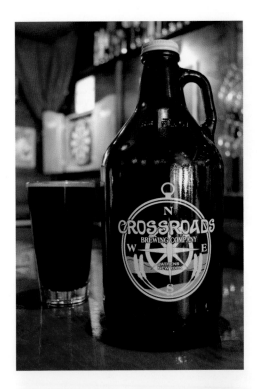

Top: A growler of Crossroad's Black Rock Stout. *Photo by Craig Gravina.*

Left: Chatham Brewery's 8-Barrel Super IPA. *Photo by Craig Gravina.*

Second Street in 1881. William also was involved in Quandts Brewery in Troy. George's two other brothers were also brewers—Septimus in New York City and John at National Brewery in Syracuse. John would eventually buy into that brewery, and Septimus would take the helm at the Hudson brewery. In Albany, Granger teamed up with maltster George Story in 1884 in a partnership that would continue until Granger's death in 1891. Story, however, would only operate the brewery for two years after his partner's death.

Another new participant, the George F. Weber Brewery and Weber-Star Bottling Works, illustrates how beer in the late 1800s was not simply a debate between strong ale and lighter lager. While the massive influx of immigrants into New York from Germany in the second half of the nineteenth century brought lager, it also brought Bavarian-style wheat beer. At least two weiss bier brewers operated in Albany during this period—George F. Weber and Cook & Meutch. The latter operated only for a short period between 1882 and 1887. Weber, however, far exceeded that. In 1858, George F. Weber's father opened a brewery and a small bottling facility in Roundout, New York, a since leveled area on the waterfront of Kingston, New York. By 1872, the operation had relocated to South Pearl Street in Albany. Two years later, the bottling facility was moved to Fourth Avenue.

As with earlier eras, the late nineteenth century saw the opening of a number of small breweries. Some succeeded while others did not. Among these small, late nineteenth-century breweries were Gregory BeBee, W.J. Dickson, Alexander Gregory, Marshall & Rapp, J.G. Schneider and William Schindler. Unusual to the time, the last two breweries—Schneider and Schindler—were owned and operated by the widows of the founders.

One of the most important brewing events in the late 1800s was not related to the opening of a new brewery or the introduction of a new technology. In 1886, the old Taylor brewery on the waterfront built in 1851 was heavily damaged in a fire. The *New York Times* reported the calamity in an article dated June 22, 1886:

> *At 6:30 o'clock this evening fire was discovered in the old Taylor brewery, one of the landmarks of the city. The building was a six-story brick structure 200 feet long by 111 feet wide. It had a capacity of about 250,000 barrels per year. Before the firemen could get to work the building was enveloped in flames. A general alarm was sounded, which brought out the entire Fire Department. At 7 o'clock a portion of the rear wall fell in, and several firemen had a narrow escape from being buried under the debris.*

The article goes on to state that the twenty thousand bushels of barley in the building were a total loss but that several hundred barrels of ale were saved. The building was stated to have been designed to be fireproof.

The year of the great fire was also the bicentennial of the Dongan Charter of 1686 establishing the autonomous municipal rights that founded the city and county of Albany. As part of the celebration, a multivolume book entitled *Bi-centennial History of Albany: History of the County of Albany, N.Y., from 1609 to 1886* was published that canvassed all aspects of life in Albany over that time. A separate chapter was included that set out the impressive history of brewing in the region as well as the state of brewing at the time of publication. We are told that ale production in 1883 totaled 236,491 barrels while in the next year the total jumped to 263,459 barrels. In addition to that, 95,743 barrels of lager were produced in 1883, a figure not quite matched by the 94,475 barrels produced the following year.

Nineteenth-century breweries' actual annual production was often about 20 to 25 percent less than their reported capacities. A brewery with a capacity to produce 100,000 barrels in reality often only produced 80,000 to 75,000 barrels during any given year. Having the space and ability to produce a specific amount of beer did not necessarily translate to that number year to year. However, it is reasonable to expect brewers built their facilities with the assumption of future growth.

The book also describes the maltsters of Albany, including the firm of John G. White & Sons, which produced 450,000 barrels of malt locally and which was discussed earlier. Another large malting firm was the house of J.W. Tillinghast. It was founded in 1850 by a Mr. John Tweddle before being taken over by Tillinghast in 1870. The firm had two separate production facilities, one located at 105 Montgomery Street and the other on the corner of State and Lark Streets. The Montgomery Street plant was five stories tall while the other building stood three stories. Together, the annual output of the firm reached approximately 300,000 bushels of malt. The operation relied on steam power and employed thirty, as did Thomas McCredie's firm. McCredie had built his production since opening in 1847 to 250,000 bushels in each year. He employed twenty-five workers at four different locations. A newer entrant to the market was Story Brothers, founded in 1868. This brewery produced 175,000 by the mid-1880s and employed fifteen.

In addition to the ill-fated Taylor brewery, the capacities of Albany's other largest breweries are also described. The Boyd brewery was by then called the Albany Brewing Company, and its brick buildings covered the block

George I. Amsdell Brewery workers, circa 1895. *Courtesy of the Albany Institute of History & Art.*

bounded by Arch, Green, South Ferry and Franklin Streets, its tallest tower reaching eight stories high. The brewery had the capacity to produce over 150,000 barrels of ale and porter annually. The firm malted 200,000 on its own each year and employed 125 workers. The president of the brewery, John S. Boyd, was the grandson of the founder.

Even the sorts of beers being brewed are described by the author of the *Bi-Centennial History*. George I. and Theodore M. Amsdell Brothers also continued brewing IPA, XX ale, Burton and stock, as well as porter, in the mid-1880s. They employed a greater number of workers, at 150, than Albany Brewing but produced almost half the beer, at eighty thousand barrels annually. Other smaller operations included the Fort Orange Brewing Company (formerly Smyth & Walker and, before that, Kirk Brewery) and the brewery of James K. Carroll and Duncan McDonald located at 900 to 912 Broadway, which manufactured India pale ale XXX, amber XX, cream ales, pale XXX, stock ales and porter.

As might be expected from this era with its wide range of styles for the ale-drinking public, the reputation of Albany ale was fading. In 1886, in a

A billhead from the Quinn & Nolan Brewery, circa 1890s. *From the collection of Aaron Connor.*

book on grammar, it was still possible to write as an example of the proper usage when writing a list of plurals:

> *I cannot but regard a certain use of the plural, as "ales, wines, teas," "woolens, silks, cottons," as a sort of traders' cant, and to many persons it is very offensive. What reason is there for a man who deals in malt liquor announcing that he has a fine stock of ales on hand, when what he has is a stock of ale of various kinds? What he means is that he has Bass's ale, and Burton ale, and Albany ale, and others; but these are only different kinds of one thing.*

Just thirteen years later, however, the beer appeared to be something largely in the past. We can see this in those recollections of ninety-six-year-old Charles H. Haswell published in the *New York Times* in 1899 as part of the newspaper's end-of-the-century retrospective. When he stated that "Albany Ale was the beverage then that lager beer is today, and a mighty good drink it was," he was only recalling a fond memory of his youth.

NINETEENTH-CENTURY BREWING IN TROY AND SCHENECTADY

By the second quarter of the nineteenth century, Albany, the largest city in the Upper Hudson Valley, had become the de facto brewing center for the region. However, ten miles north, the city of Troy, its northern neighbor Lansingburgh and West Troy (now Watervilet) directly across the river had developed successful brewing industries in their own right. According to *Papers Relative to the Tariffs Published in the United States in the Years 1824 and 1828*, prepared by the Great Britain Foreign Office, by the late 1820s, Troy was exporting twelve thousand barrels of ale annually, a modest number, but respectable for an area with a population of under ten thousand people.

Although Stephen Schuyler had operated his brew house during the 1790s, the first brewery to open in the city during the nineteenth century came sixteen years later when Charles Hurstfield and Thomas Tranor built a brewery on the corner of Ferry Street and Sixth Avenue. Thomas Read and his partner, Sterling Armstrong, purchased the brewery in 1823. Read and eventually his sons would continue to run it quite successfully until 1867. The Nash family, however, owned perhaps the most successful of the early Troy breweries.

In 1817, Connecticut-native Abraham Nash Jr. established a brewery on what would become Fifth Avenue in Troy. Nash's son Alfred joined his father in business in 1833, as did, for a short time, the Albany brewer Uri Burt. By the late 1830s, the Burt partnership had dissolved, but the brewery had become so successful that it was determined that a depot needed to be established in New York City. By 1845, the Nashes and their new partner, the former head of their New York depot, Ebeneezer Beadleston, purchased the old state prison in what is now Greenwich Village, converting it into a second brewing facility.

Troy was growing into one of the most prosperous and industrial cities in the United States. Henry Burden's ironworks became a driving force behind the city's industrialization. Steel and iron produced in the city was often used at the federal arsenal across the river in West Troy. Like in Albany, the opening of the Erie Canal also help to boost the city's success during the first half of the nineteenth century. From 1820 to 1850, the city saw a nearly 450 percent increase in its population. Its brewing industry followed suit. Samuel Bolton opened his brewery in Lansingburgh in 1865; his brother William joined the firm nine years later.

During the late nineteenth century, Troy became one of the most industrial and prosperous cities in the country. Troy's anchor industry, ironworking, had grown extensively during and after the American Civil War, as did its brewing industry. By the 1880s, Troy had nine operating breweries in it—second only to Albany in the Upper Hudson Valley. *Courtesy of the Library of Congress.*

The Nashes' brewing interests continued to expand. Abraham and Alfred Nash helmed their northern brewery from Troy while Beadleston operated the southern interest. Both breweries operated jointly as Nash, Beadleston & Co. until 1856. That year, Alfred assumed control of the Troy brewery—renaming it A.B. Nash & Co.—but still retained an interest in the Manhattan facility. Although Alfred listed his occupation as brewer, he had become increasingly involved with the State Bank of Troy, taking a position as one of its directors a few years earlier. Nash retired in 1860, and the New York Brewery was reorganized between Beadleston and his new partners. Within five years of his retirement, Nash sold the Troy brewery to Irishmen James Daley and John Stanton.

During the first fifty years of the nineteenth century, Albany saw an influx of English- and Scottish-born brewers move into the city. Troy, however, would see an Irish influence. Kyran Cleay was one of the earliest of the city's Irish brewers, opening his brewery with his partner, Edward Murphy, in 1844. Fellow Irishmen James Lundy, William Kennedy and Daniel Dunn were involved with a number of brewing interests in the city alone and sometimes with one another during the 1850s and '60s. In 1867, Edward Murphy Jr., son of the Murphy in business with Kyran Cleary, partnered with William Kennedy in what had originally been the Read Brewery. Kennedy had purchased the brewery with Daniel Dunn earlier in the year but changed partners shortly thereafter.

This proliferation of Irish brewers continued in Troy for the next twenty years. While in the earlier part of the century, most of these brewers were Irish, by the 1870s and '80s, Irish American brewers became common in the city. A prime example of this was the Troy-born Conway brothers and their partner, Nicholas Kane, who purchased what had been the Sands brewery in 1883. The most successful of these Irish breweries, however, was Fitzgerald Brothers and Stanton Breweries.

With Dunn and Kennedy and later Murphy moving to their new location on Ferry Street, Michael, John and Edmund Fitzgerald purchased the old brewery on River Street. Michael left the partnership in 1870, leaving his two brothers to oversee the building of their new brewery, the Garryowen Brewery, built between 1877 and 1881 at the same location on River Street. The new brewery produced both ale and lager. John and Edmund continued to grow their business together until John's death in 1885. His son Thomas and nephew A.T. Fitzpatrick joined Edmund during the 1890s. The firm was rebranded officially as Fitzgerald Brothers by 1895 and continued to operate well into the twentieth century.

John Stanton and James Daley, who had purchased the Nash Brewery in 1865, continued their partnership until 1880, when Daley went his own way. He left to open the Phoenix Brewery on Second Street, a firm that at one time had been the Troy Brewing Company. Stanton stayed the course and saw his sons William and Edmond join the family business, now called simply the John Stanton Brewery. Like Fitzgerald Brothers, Stanton made both ale and lager as well as porter.

Irish brewers were a large part of Troy's brewing industry but were not the sole nonnative group to affect the city's beer. Brewers who immigrated from Central Europe and what would become Germany played a significant role in Troy's beer making, as well. Like the majority of the country, but unlike Albany, Troy embraced lager production. Although the city continued to produce some ale, notably from the Stanton and Bolton breweries, by early the twentieth century, most of the city's breweries were producing lager.

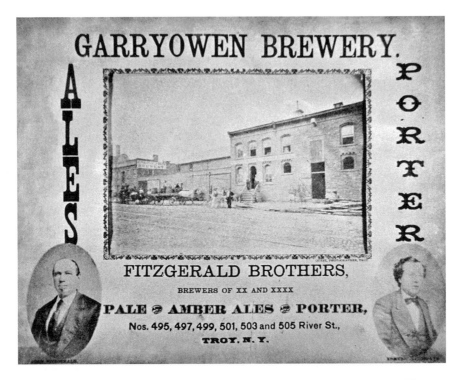

One of the most successful of Troy Irish-owned breweries was Fitzgerald Brothers. The brothers opened what was originally know as the Garryowen Brewery in 1877, and it would continue to operate until 1962. *Courtesy of Brown's Brewing Company.*

Christian Isengart, Jacob Stoll, A. Louis Ruscher and Leo Kirchner all opened small lager breweries in the city during the 1850s. Stoll and Ruscher partnered with each other starting in 1855, even though Ruscher was also running his own brewery. Their partnership lasted until the mid-1860s, when Stoll purchased George Koob's lager operation on Spring Street. Leo Kirchner—apparently no relation to Albany's Jacob Kirchner—brewed lager in Troy for eighteen years before the Quandt brothers, Andrew and Adam, purchased his brewery. Quandt in turn was eventually purchased by Bolton Brewery in the late nineteenth century and would continue producing lager under the Quandt name while Bolton made ale and porter.

Isengart, like his central European brethren before him, opened his lager brewery on Tenth Street and the Hoosick Street hill. Isengart is perhaps the best brewery to illustrate Troy's multicultural brewing heritage. After Christian Isengart's death, his widow, Elizabeth, partnered with two Troy-born businessmen of Irish heritage—William Donohue and Michael

Tierney—forming Donohue-Tierney-Isengart Brewing Company. All these breweries were still operating at the turn of the twentieth century.

Although Schenectady, less than twenty miles northwest of either Troy or Albany, is considered part of the Upper Hudson Valley, its culture and population identify themselves more with the Mohawk Valley and the counties of New York's Leatherstocking region than they do with their eastern counterparts. Until the end of the nineteenth century, it was also significantly smaller than either Troy or Albany.

Albany and Troy grew first due to their connection with the Hudson River, both cities expanding in a somewhat symbiotic relationship with the river. Schenectady, on the other hand, was born of an exodus away from the Hudson when Arent van Curler led his band of followers into New York's western frontier in the 1660s. The city's brewing history faced west with the brewing Vrooman family moving deeper into the frontier from Schenectady into the Schoharie Valley in the first half of the 1700s. When the canal arrived in the 1820s, Troy and Albany saw themselves as linkage points between western raw ingredients and points south. Schenectady, however, embraced its location as the man-made waterway's first true inland depot on the artificial river heading to the new west.

Schenectady's brewing industry after the Revolution and into the new century was negligible compared to Albany and Troy. By the 1820s and early 1830s, the city's first ward saw the opening of a few brew houses. Most notable from this period was John Moffat, who operated in Schenectady after opening a brewery in Geneva, New York, with Walter Grieve in the 1790s. Having returned east in the teens, Moffat brewed in Schenectady until the late 1820s, when he and his son headed west again, opening what was perhaps the first brewery in Buffalo. A "Mr. LeBritton"—mentioned in Howell and Munsell's *History of the County of Schenecatdy, N.Y., from 1662 to 1886*—also brewed in the city for a short time. This may well have been Edward Le Breton, having returned to the Upper Hudson Valley from New York City.

The area in what is now the city's historic Stockade neighborhood, along Union Street, became the hub for the Schenectady brewing into the mid-nineteenth century—including breweries owned by John Vrooman, Issac Schermerhorn and Francis Myers. By the 1860s, malt houses also became a common sight in the little city. Moving into the later nineteenth century, like in Troy, those few breweries operating in Schenectady began focusing on lager rather than ale. Albert Schinnerer was making lager at his Centre Street Brewery. Schinnerer partnered with and then sold the brewery to Jospeh Meyers in the mid-1870s. The brewery continued into the early 1880s. Peter Engel followed suit in 1874, also making lager at his Nott Terrace Brewery.

Schenectady's biggest growth came with the arrival of Thomas Edison. The inventor and scientist moved his machine works to the city in 1887. This relocation would become a major economic force as Edison's company developed into the fourth largest in the world—General Electric. With this new infusion of both money and population into the city, Schenectady saw the opening—and, in most cases, the closing in quick succession—of a few more breweries through the 1890s and early twentieth century. The most successful was started by John Dunn, who opened what would become the Mohawk Valley Brewing Company on Dock Street (later Foster Avenue) in 1893. Mohawk Valley was the last brewery to operate in the Electric City, closing before 1914, all but ending Schenectady's brewery history.

THE REGION AT THE END OF THE 1800S

The nineteenth century saw the culmination of large-scale brewing in the United States. In New York's Upper Hudson Valley, breweries that started as small operations grew rapidly in the first fifty years of the century. Those small breweries produced hundreds, then thousands, then hundreds of thousands of barrels of beer—nearly overnight—growing into major industrial facilities.

Early in the century, they capitalized on New York's agricultural resources and then exploited the largest engineering accomplishment of the time—the Erie Canal. The Upper Hudson area's ale and lager producers were at the forefront of the Industrial Revolution—first using steam to power their boats and move their beer hundreds of miles in a single day and then to power the breweries themselves. Even the American Civil War, the country's bloodiest conflict, couldn't deter the rise of brewing in the Upper Hudson Valley. By the end of the century, commercial refrigeration changed production brewing forever. It forced a shift from the old traditions of ale making to new brewing techniques brought by waves of central European immigrants.

The nineteenth century was, without doubt, a brewer's century, riding the wave of wealth, progress and technological advances. Not that deep into the twentieth century, much of this promise and industry would disappear.

5
1900 to the Present Day

The early twentieth century was a time of flux for the breweries of the Upper Hudson Valley. The massive numbers of immigrants from central and Eastern Europe coming into New York had brought not only a demand for lager but also new brewing techniques that began infiltrating what were once traditionally English-style ale breweries. Organized labor and unions were becoming a notable force in both the malting and brewing industries. Consolidation and the purchasing of smaller breweries by larger breweries or brewing conglomerates had become quite common. The notion of a buyout of American breweries by foreign investors—including the so-called English Syndicate of British businessmen—loomed on the horizon just as the ever-present clamor of national Prohibition and the temperance movement grew louder with each year.

By the turn of the twentieth century, the large lager breweries of New York City and the Midwest dominated the beer market in the United States. To compete in the era of rail and industry, breweries needed to produce at least 100,000 barrels per year. Almost none of the Upper Hudson Valley breweries were capable of doing this by the first decade of the new century. There were a few exceptions, such as Michael Nolan's dual venture, Beverwyck and Quinn & Nolan; the Albany Brewing Company; and the Bolton/Quandt conglomerate in Troy.

THE BEGINNING OF THE END FOR ALBANY'S BREWERS

No new breweries opened in Albany in the thirty-year period between 1890 and 1920. While ale production remained high, lager production was also increasing. Albany ale had nearly vanished by the beginning of the twentieth century. By 1905, George I. Amsdell Brewing Co. was likely the only brewery still making a beer branded as Albany Ale. The Taylor Brewery continued to operate at Broadway and Arch until it closed in 1905. The building burned again in 1914, but two years later, Albany Hardware & Iron Co. would rebuild in nearly the same footprint as the old brewery. That building still stands as the iconic U-Haul building in downtown Albany.

The early years of the 1900s saw more mergers and acquisitions in the name of industrial progress. New money was coming into the region. In 1905, a plan to syndicate twelve of the breweries operating along the Hudson River from Albany to Troy began to take form. Initiated, most likely, as a tactic to stave off the risk of British investors snapping them up, the strategy was spearheaded by George C. Hawley, partner and son-in-law of the recently deceased Theodore Amsdell. This conglomeration of both ale and lager breweries was to be named the Hudson Valley Breweries Company. The new company would be helmed by Hawley and headquartered in Albany. Along with the conglomeration, the intent was to close a few of the smaller operations and focus efforts on the higher outputting facilities. However, in-fighting and conflicting egos dogged the measure, and as is said, the best-laid plans of mice and men oft go astray.

Ale brewing was changing at this time, too, as Amsdell's Albany XX Ale of 1901 illustrates. Stylistically, the "proto" Albany ale–like beers of Mathew Vassar and Thomas Read that were made in the 1830s were strong—well past 9 percent alcohol by volume—pale and used the bare minimum of fermentables, mainly pale malt and honey. Seventy years later, Amsdell's version of Albany ale was weaker—hovering around 5 percent ABV—and copper-hued due to the addition of black malt. Amsdell's brew also incorporated more ingredients than the earlier 1830s beers. Pale malt was used, but corn—which would become a major component of American brewing in the twentieth century—made up a good portion of the Amsdell grist in 1901. The honey of the earlier beers was also replaced with processed brewing sugars and glucose.

Amsdell logs, held in the collection of the Albany Institute of History & Art, also show that the process by which turn-of-the-century ale was made

The one-time largest brewery in the country Taylor Brewery was a shell of its former self by 1903. Most of its buildings had been sold off, including its malt house, which had been sold to the Albany Brewing Co. years earlier. The Taylor family was no longer associated with the brewery; only their name remained. The brewery would close two years after this photo was taken, and the building would burn to the ground in 1914. *Courtesy of the Albany Institute of History & Art.*

Taking advantage of travelers' taste for lager, Beverwyck, Dobler and Hinckel (not shown), the city's largest producer of such, advertised along the Albany Basin. This image shows the State Street pier at the turn of the twentieth century. Passenger trains heading to Union Station and boats traveling on the Hudson River passed by these signs daily. *Courtesy of the Albany Institute of History & Art.*

were changing too. It's clear when reading the Amsdell logs that German lager-brewing techniques were influencing ale production by the turn of the twentieth century. Amsdell's beers were not parti-gyled, like Vassar's had been; they were, however, *kräusened*, a technique in which unfermented wort is added to beer for carbonating and conditioning purposes. Additionally, Amsdell's Polar Ale, a cream ale–like beer in the brewery's lineup, was cold conditioned over beechwood chips. All of these methods stem from traditionally German styles of beer making.

The Upper Hudson industrial breweries, like those anywhere, were always inherently dangerous places to work. Aside from the constant threat of fire, heavy casks and malfunctioning machinery crushed legs and arms. Pressurized barrels and kegs often exploded, sending iron hoop and oak stave splinters rocketing through the close quarters of the brewery, like shrapnel from a grenade. Two brewery workers were killed, and two others were injured at James Quinn's Albany brewery during an 1865 explosion that caused $25,000 in damages to the building. Although late nineteenth- and early twentieth-century breweries had adapted many safety procedures, danger was still

At the turn of the twentieth century, a technique of enveloping metal in a thin layer of porcelain, which could easily be printed on, was developed for making weatherproof, exterior signage. This application also offered a new advertising venue for breweries—the waterproof beer tray, although most were used for decoration rather than as trays. This tray is emblazoned with Hinckel Brewery's stag emblem. *From the collection of Aaron Connor.*

present and even increased with industrialization. In 1901, a ruptured steam header killed two men at the Bartholomay Brewery in Rochester.

Accidents were not the only cause of death or injury in turn-of-the-century breweries. The Bolton Brewery was the scene of another gruesome incident. The Bolton family had owned and operated their brewery in Lansingburg since 1865. Samuel Bolton Sr. had opened the brewery, but by the turn of the twentieth century, his son Samuel Jr. had taken over day-to-day operations. In their nearly forty-year tenure, the Boltons had amassed a sizable fortune; unfortunately, the younger Bolton's later investment choices may not have been all that sound. On May 9, 1901, a worker found Bolton's wallet, hat, coat and watch near one of the brewery's coppers. Upon closer inspection, his body was found floating in the vat of boiling wort. His suicide was believed to have been a result of heavy losses in the stock market.

Consolidations continued to define the industry in this era. George Amsdell continued to run Amsdell Brewing & Malting Company until his death in 1906, when the principal owners of the much smaller Kirchner Brewery bought the brewery out from under the Amsdell family. The brewery was again renamed, this time Amsdell-Kirchner Brewery, but fell into bankruptcy shortly thereafter. In 1909, a New Hampshire–based company bought the brewery but continued to run it as Amsdell-Kirchner until it was sold once again to the New York City conglomerate Knickerbocker Brewing Corporation. The Amsdell-Kirchner Brewery closed just before the start of national Prohibition. The original brewery building on Jay Street was converted first to a hotel and later apartments. That apartment complex, the Knickerbocker, still stands in the Center Square neighborhood of Albany.

A series of brewing conglomerates would also purchase what had been Smyth & Walker, now known as the Fort Orange Brewing Company. It would become the Municipal Brewing Co. and then the Capitol Brewing Co. during the 1890s. Then as part of the Knickerbocker Brewing Corporation, it closed in 1916 under the name of Consumers Brewing Company. Like the Fort Orange Brewing Company, the Albany Brewing Company was also bought and sold by a number of brewing consolidators and was eventually also purchased by Kinckerbocker, as well. Like Consumers, it, too, was closed in 1916, after 120 years in operation.

By the first decade of the twentieth century, Hedrick Brewing was one of the smallest breweries operating in the city of Albany. By 1910, it was only capable of producing ten thousand barrels per year. Purchased by Knickerbocker, it suffered the same fate as Amsdell-Kirchner, Consumers and the Albany Brewing Company and closed in 1916. It was, however, reopened in the early 1920s by a group of local investors, who planned to make a nonalcoholic malt and apple drink.

Similarly, George F. Weber helmed the Weber Brewery alone until 1906, when his brother August joined the firm. Renaming the company A.C. & G.F. Weber, it was at this time that the brothers would begin to seriously focus on their bottling business. By 1915, the now Weber-Star Bottling Works was bottling for a number of breweries and soda makers across New York State. The Webers' brewing business ceased due to national Prohibition, but their bottling facility continued well into the 1950s.

Unlike Hedrick and Weber, there was no short-term salvation for the Evans Brewery. Upon Cornealius Evans's death in 1902, ownership transferred to

"Evans Ale" emblazoned on the Evans Brewery became a well-known sight to travelers along the Hudson River. By the early 1900s, the brewery had grown from a small, one- or two-building operation to a sprawling complex along the river, having become one of the best-known breweries in the Hudson Valley. *Courtesy of Historic Hudson, Rowles Collection.*

his two sons—Cornealius Jr. and Robert—his partners since the late 1880s. The brothers continued to operate the Hudson, New York brewery with great success. But like nearly everyone else, by 1920, they were also forced to close due to Prohibition. Its name, however, would be heard again.

Dobler continued under Amsdell's leadership until his death in 1902. The brewery struggled, until being bought by Feigenspan Brewing Co. of Newark, New Jersey, in 1908. The Feigenspan family had operated their brewery in Newark since the mid-1870s, and by the first decade of the twentieth century, it had exceeded its capacity. Christian W. Feigenspan, son of the founder, assumed the presidency of the Newark brewery in 1907 and facilitated the purchase of Dobler a year later. The Dobler Brewery of Albany would begin making a similar lineup of beers as its parent operation in New Jersey and, under that ownership, found a way to survive the upcoming dry years.

Michael Nolan died in 1905, having built his breweries into the largest facilities in the Upper Hudson Valley and the only ones seriously capable of competing on a national level. By the early twentieth century, the breweries were producing hundreds of thousands of barrels per year—with Quinn & Nolan still producing ale and Beverwyck making lager. The facilities would stop producing beer throughout the thirteen years of Prohibition but would also find a way to go on.

Dobler Brewery workers, 1908. *Photo courtesy of Charlene Dreimiller and family.*

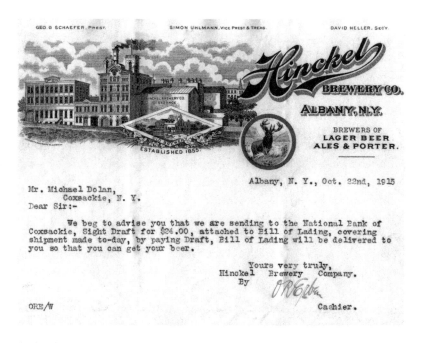

A 1915 letterhead from the Hinckel Brewery. Note the image of Hinckel's original brewery in the diamond inset. *From the collection of Aaron Connor.*

The years between the end of the 1800s and the beginning of national Prohibition saw a great reduction in the number of breweries in the Upper Hudson. Eleven breweries were in operation in Albany at the turn-of-the-century: Beverwyck, Quinn & Nolan, Amsdell, Taylor, Weber, Dobler, Hedrick, Kirchner, Consumer's Brewing Co., Albany Brewing Company and Hinckle. By 1919, and the ratification of the Eighteenth Amendment prohibiting the sale, production and transportation of alcohol, the number had dropped to four: Beverwyck, making lager; Quinn & Nolan, producing ale; and Dobler and Hinckle, making both. With the peak of political success for the temperance movement coming, there was little to suggest this trend would not continue.

PROHIBITION, DAN O'CONNELL AND LEGS DIAMOND

Calls for national Prohibition in the United States had echoed throughout the marbled walls of Washington, D.C., for years. After two attempts, in 1913 and 1915, finally, in December 1917, Congress approved a resolution to amend the U.S. Constitution—in what would become the Eighteenth Amendment—to forbid "the manufacture, sale, or transportation of intoxicating liquors within, the importation thereof into, or the exportation thereof from the United States and all territory subject to the jurisdiction thereof for beverage purposes."

By January 1916, thirty-six states had ratified the amendment, followed by Congress three years later to the day—officially making the Eighteenth Amendment federal law. Supported and enforced by the Volstead Act, national Prohibition went into effect on January 17, 1920. If graft and corruption concerning politics and alcohol were bad at the end of the nineteenth century, the enactment of national Prohibition completely changed the game.

Albany and the Upper Hudson Valley were affected by Prohibition just as every other city in the United States was. By law, the production, transportation and sale of alcohol was illegal. Because of that, Albany saw its share of illegally produced "bootleg" alcohol as well its fair share of speakeasies. As a capital city, the demand for alcohol by powerful political figures was high. Being located halfway between the Canadian border and New York City on U.S. Routes 9 and 20 also made the area

ESTABLISHED 1858

A Delightfully Refreshing Beverage

STAR GINGER ALE

Cascade Ginger Ale
Wards Orange, Lemon,
Lime Crush and Cherry

HOPS

BOTTLE CAPS AND BOTTLES

MALT SYRUP

WEBER
Star Bottling Works

76-82 THIRD AVENUE
ALBANY, N. Y.

TELEPHONE MAIN 898

The Weber family had abandoned brewing prior to Prohibition to focus on their bottling operations. However, this circa 1924 Albany and Rensselaer City Directory ad for Weber Star Bottling Works offers malt syrup and hops—a nod to the company's brewing history—alongside its brand of Ginger Ale and various other sodas bottled at the facility. *Albany Institute of History & Art.*

a stopover for whiskey leaving Canada on the old trade route bound for New York City, Boston, New Jersey and Philadelphia. The Upper Hudson valley was, for lack of a better term, "wet" with strong alcoholic spirits like gin and whiskey.

Beer, however, was another story. Because of its low alcohol content, beer can't be so easily cut with water or spiked with another form of alcohol without the drinker noticing. At the time, to be profitable, beer had to be made in large quantities and, therefore, required large facilities to make it. Large facilities are hard to hide from Prohibition officers and other law enforcement officials.

In response, Beverwyck began operating as Beverwyck Co. Inc. and closed its ale-producing counterpart, Quinn & Nolan, to focus on making malt vinegar, near beer and soda. Feigenspan Brewery, the parent company to Albany's Dobler Brewing Co., shut down its brewing operation in Newark and converted its original brewery for use in ice and coal production, but it kept its sign lit throughout the entire thirteen years of Prohibition in silent, yet glowing protest. In Albany, Feigenspan kept Dobler open and produced near beer and soda.

Hedrick Brewing Co. was the exception to this—a big exception. Initially, Hedrick closed but was purchased by a group of local businessmen, who appeared to be operating the business legally making a nonalcoholic concoction of apples and malt. They were, in fact, bootlegging. Producing beer and pumping it out through the basement of the brewery. They were eventually caught and prosecuted in the mid-1920s. Former Albany County district attorney John J. Conway defended the group, taking ownership of the brewery in lieu of owed legal fees. Conway was a close friend of the Albany County Democratic Committee head, political boss and ultimately driving force behind Albany's nearly sixty-year Democratic machine—Daniel P. O'Connell.

O'Connell, who came from nothing and grew up in Albany's south end, had been elected in 1919 as city assessor but quit a few years later to head the Democratic Party in Albany. From that point, he and his cronies, including O'Connell's brother Ed and the longest-termed mayor in the history of the United States, Erastus Corning II, ran Albany like Capone ran Chicago. O'Connell's power wasn't limited to just Albany either. His Democratic machine had links to both the New York State capitol and Washington, D.C. As one of the dominant political forces in New York, O'Connell had deep influence—both legal and illegal. Along with the polling places and political patronage, O'Connell controlled Albany's police force, red-light district, gambling, bootlegging and, with Conway's acquisition of Hedrick Brewing, its beer. Hedrick continued producing illegal, full-strength beer after Conway assumed ownership, and although Conway owned the brewery, its profits benefited O'Connell. The last thing O'Connell was going to allow was competition—be it in politics or booze—and he did an amazing job of keeping out both the Republicans and the rackets out of Albany.

However, in 1931, John Moran—better known as Jack "Legs" Diamond—showed up in the city. Diamond, the flamboyant associate of the recently murdered Manhattan gambler and racketeer Arnold Rothstein, was attempting to expand his former boss's booze and crime empire up the Hudson River. This expansion did not go unnoticed by the other mobsters in New York. Since the late 1920s, Diamond had been in a turf war with a Bronx-based gangster, Dutch Schultz, a war that resulted in a number of lead slugs being pulled from Diamond's body. In 1930, Diamond—having recently been kicked out of Europe, when officials there realized he was on the hunt for narcotics and booze—was shot at the Hotel Monticello on the West Side of Manhattan. The gunmen peppered him with four rounds. He recovered, but by that point, Schultz had moved from the Bronx into Diamond's territory in Manhattan. Diamond new it was time to get out of New York. He and his crew set up shop at the Aratoga Inn, in Cairo, New York, a tiny hamlet an hour's drive south of Albany.

Rural Greene County was the perfect place to pinch the supply of booze moving from Canada to New York City. It was secluded, which made hiding liquor easy, yet close enough to Albany to satisfy Diamond's insatiable appetite for the nightlife. Diamond was becoming a celebrity. The press glorified his antics. They portrayed him as a gentleman gangster, a daring, Robin Hood–like character—stealing from the rich and giving hooch to the poor. In reality, that was far from the truth. Diamond was a brutal killer, and he laid claim to the "whiskey highway" with a vengeance. In the spring of 1930, Diamond beat a truck driver he believed was running hard cider. Shortly thereafter, he kidnapped and tortured a local bootlegger named Jack Duncan. Arrested for both assaults in the spring of 1931, he was tried and acquitted on the first charge, but the charges of kidnapping and torture wouldn't be so easy to avoid. The law wasn't Diamond's only problem, either. Six days after his arrest, a gunman sunk three bullets into Diamond while he was eating dinner at the Aratoga. Again, he recovered. The acquittal and attack only bolstered Diamond's reputation as the unconvictable, unkillable gentleman gangster.

During Diamond's recovery, New York State Troopers raided his headquarters in Cairo, recovering $5,000 worth of illegal alcohol—which added federal bootlegging charges to his list of crimes. In August 1931, Diamond and his lieutenant Paul Quattrocchi were tried on violations against the Volstead Act and sentenced to four years in prison. Diamond appealed the conviction. Within a few weeks, Diamond's kidnapping case began. His savvy lawyer, Daniel Prior, petitioned to have his trial moved from Catskill to Troy, New York. Prior seriously doubted a conviction from a Rensselaer County jury enamored of Diamond's charming ways and reputation. Out

This photo from 1931 shows a gaunt, Jack "Legs" Diamond (second from left) after he had been released from the hospital, having been shot three times by a gunman at the Aratoga Inn in Cairo. *Courtesy of the Boston Public Library, Leslie Jones Collection.*

on bail and biding his time during the federal appeals process, Diamond set up shop at the Kenmore Hotel in Albany. Diamond used the hotel's Rain-Bo Room like his own personal living room, dancing, womanizing and playing the hotel's piano well into the night.

Obviously, a man in Dan O'Connell's position did not like having such a high-profile threat to his empire cavorting the night away at one of his city's premier establishments. O'Connell tolerated the gangster at first and actually arranged for police protection for him at the hotel. But when rumors that Diamond had plans to get into the beer and extortion business in Albany arose, tensions escalated.

Prior was right—Diamond was acquitted of the kidnapping charge. On December 17, 1931, Jack Diamond was free and clear, and the federal charge of bootlegging was under appeal. The world was Diamond's oyster. He headed straight for the Kenmore and spent most of the evening celebrating there with friends. He left around 1:00 a.m., stopping first at his mistress's (Kiki Roberts) place, before going home to his Dove Street apartment. Just before dawn on the morning of the eighteenth, three shots rang out. Legs Diamond, the unkillable killer, was found face down in his bed with three bullets in his skull.

Rumors abounded about the killing of America's favorite gangster. Suspects included his biggest rival, Dutch Schultz; Arnold Rothstein's protégé, Charlie Luciano; and the Philadelphia bootlegger Waxey Gordon. The most accepted theory, however, is that O'Connell had Diamond killed for trying to move in on his bootlegging and beer operations. William "Doc" Fitzpatrick—a friend of O'Connell's and an Albany police sergeant and future chief of police—was most likely the triggerman. Diamond was dead, and the official repeal of Prohibition went into effect almost exactly two years later, on December 15, 1933.

Post-Prohibition Albany Beer

As was mentioned, Dobler continued to operate during the Prohibition years as the soda and near beer–making operation for the Feigenspan family. After repeal, Dobler recommenced standard brewing, essentially making the same beer as Feigenspan in New Jersey. During the 1930s, Dobler adopted Feigenspan's slogan P.O.N, but rather than the New Jersey–centric "Pride of Newark," the Albany brewery opted for its version to represent the "Pride of the Nation."

Feigenspan Jr. died in 1939, and within four years, his brewery—at that point one of the largest in the country—was purchased by its neighbor, P. Ballantine & Sons Brewing Co. Dobler, however, was not part of that purchase and

Dobler thrived early in the post-repeal era. It had remained open during Prohibition, making near beer for its Newark, New Jersey parent, Feigenspan Brewing Company. After repeal, Dobler produced a variety of beers—both ales and lagers. Courtesy of the *Albany Institute of History & Art.*

continued on in Albany under the leadership of Edwin Feigenspan, Christian Jr.'s brother. The Feigenspan family retained ownership of Dobler, operating it until selling to Hamden-Harvard Brewery in 1959. The brewery was torn down in the early 1960s to make way for apartment housing associated with Governor Nelson Rockefeller's Empire State Plaza project. It is safe to say that had Feigenspan not purchased the Dobler Brewing Co. when it did, there most likely would have only been two breweries, rather than three, that reopened in Albany after the ratification of the Twenty-first Amendment in 1933.

From 1934 to 1949, Beverwyck was the major regional brewery in the Hudson Valley, with distribution reaching Rochester, New York City, Boston and points north to the Canadian border. It became renowned for its Irish Brand Cream Ale but produced a number of other styles, such as IPA, bock and its Golden Dry Beer—a light lager. During World War II, Beverwyck was one of forty breweries across the country contracted by U.S. Army to produce beer to be sent to American troops fighting overseas. Steel rationing halted

A Dobler "P.O.N." coaster, circa late 1930s. *From the collection of Aaron Connor.*

beer can production in 1942 but was reinstituted for these forty breweries two years later in 1944. Regional breweries, like Beverwyck in Albany, produced olive drab cans, which were then sent to areas where men from those specific areas were fighting as a way to boost morale. In the case of Beverwyck, its cans were most likely sent to Hawaii and the central Pacific—the theater of operations that many Upper Hudson Valley servicemen were fighting in with New York's Twenty-seventh Infantry Division.

Although popular locally, competition was growing for Beverwyck. The facility was purchased in 1950 by the Brooklyn-based brewery F&M Schaefer and Company. By the late-1940s, Schaefer had become one of the dominant East Coast breweries and had exceeded capacity at its New York facility. The purchase of Beverwyck would usher in an era of brewery merger and acquisition in the Upper Hudson Valley that would continue for the next twenty years. All Schaefer's local competitors—Hedrick and Dobler in Albany and Fitzgerald Brothers and Stanton Breweries in Troy—would be bought and closed by 1965.

This aerial photo shows the Beverwyck complex just after its purchase by Schaefer in 1950. The Quinn & Nolan Brewery was torn down after Prohibition and replaced with the modern L-shaped building in the middle left of the photo. However, Beverwyck's ornate brick structure is still apparent. *Courtesy of the New York State Archives.*

Schaefer underwent a major renovation and expansion between 1958 and 1966 and a modern canning facility was added in 1970—by which time the plant was nearly unrecognizable from what it had been twenty years earlier. Gone were the intricate architecture and ornate details that were a hallmark of the Beverwyck Brewery, replaced with steel, aluminum and glass. The remodeling was to no avail; the Schaefer plant in Albany only continued for two more years, when the construction of a new brewery outside Allentown, Pennsylvania, forced its closure in 1972. The brewery was razed a few years later. Some buildings were left untouched, but what was the Beverwyck complex was completely leveled. The first attempt to demolish the building failed. The demolition charges blew, and the building lurched slightly to one side but remained upright, nearly undamaged—a testament to its construction and a metaphor for the Albany brewing industry's stalwartness. What was supposed to be a relatively quick demolition ended up being a months-long hand dismantling of the brewery, brick by brick.

Of the three breweries that survived Prohibition in Albany, Hedrick was the one that seems to be the beer most associated with Albany. Ironically, Hedrick was the smallest of the three breweries—significantly smaller than Dobler and practically insignificant compared to Schaefer. It also seems to have been universally disliked. Nevertheless, Hedrick had something neither Beverwyck or Dobler had—political connections. Had Dan O'Connell not "acquired" the brewery, it most likely would not have survived Prohibition—or, quite honestly, general competition. Hedrick was the very definition of "it's not what you know; it's who you know." It was O'Connell's heavy shadow—not the beer's taste—that caused the beer's ubiquity. There is a well-known Albany adage about Hedrick: "If you didn't sell Hedrick, you didn't have a bar."

This rhetoric even made it into the 1938 New York State governor's race. The October 27, 1938 edition of the *Silver Creek News and Times* of Chautaqua County, New York, reported on a radio speech given by then Republican gubernatorial candidate and future presidential candidate Thomas Dewey.

Rallying against corruption in Brooklyn and Albany—both cities under the control of Democratic political bosses—Dewey railed against the whole of O'Connell's Machine politics in Albany and brought beer into the conversation as well. The *News and Times* reported, verbatim, Dewey's inclusion of the O'Connells' connection to the beer business and Hedrick Brewing. The paper reported that the candidate said, "When a tavern keeper puts in Hedrick's 100 per cent. The sky is the limit. He gets his license renewed without a hitch. He can have slot machines, hostesses, music and dancing. He can forget every technical regulation. He can stay open all night and throw away the key."

Opposite, top: Hedrick Brewery, by all accounts, should not have survived Prohibition. It was one of the lowest-producing lager breweries in the Upper Hudson Valley—even by Albany standards. The brewery would have remained shuttered after the repeal of Prohibition had it not been for political boss Dan O'Connell and his influence. By the late 1930s, when this photo was taken, the brewery was thriving due mostly to coercion by O'Connell's lackeys. *Albany Institute of History & Art.*

Opposite, bottom: It might be said that no two men shaped the course of Albany more than the forty-two-year mayor Erastus Corning II (left) and the Albany County Democratic Party boss Daniel P. O'Connor (right). The Albany Democratic Machine affected almost every aspect of daily life in Albany—from taxation and garbage removal to tavern licenses and beer distribution. *Courtesy of the* Times Union.

Dewey also added, "In Albany the barrooms sell Hedrick's beer—or else."
Dewey ultimately lost that election but won in 1942, holding the governorship until 1951. He continued to goad O'Connell throughout his political career. Still, O'Connell continued to run Hedrick and his Democratic machine in Albany, annoyed yet generally unaffected by his nemesis's attacks.

But everything has its time, even the pervasive Hedrick. Its name was purchased in 1965 by Piels Brothers—owned itself by Associated Brewing, as of 1963. O'Connell shuttered the brewery that same year. The brewery was torn down and eventually replaced by the Central Towers apartment building. Hedrick, like Dobler, had a life after Albany at Hamden-Harvard. The brand was sold again in 1974 to Eastern Brewing Co., of Hammonton, New Jersey. Production of Hedrick stopped when that brewery closed in 1990. Now, instead of being in every bar in the city, it is in the memories of the men and women who grew up in Albany during the height of its popularity.

Twentieth-Century Troy Brewing

In the ten years prior to the start of Prohibition, Troy had ten operating breweries. The numbers are nearly identical to Albany, a city almost two-thirds larger. By the first decade of the twentieth century, Stanton, in particular, was doing quite well for itself. When John Stanton died in 1917, Stanton Brewery—and its previous incarnation—had already been brewing beer for one hundred years.

Troy was a bawdy town during the thirteen years of Prohibition. The O'Connell Democratic machine kept a tight reign on Albany, but the brothers' coercive influence didn't reach as far north as the Collar City. Troy, almost dead center between New York City and the Canadian border, also was a perfect stopover for bootleggers transporting illegal alcohol to the large American cities of the Northeast.

The city's more lenient attitude toward alcohol may have contributed to the success of its three breweries—Stanton, Quandt and Fitzgerald Brothers—to survive the dark years. All three breweries reopened and resumed brewing operations well past repeal. Quandt closed in 1942, Stanton eight years later in 1950—having operated for 133 years—and Fitzgerald Brothers in 1962. Coincidentally, both the Stanton and Fitzgerald Brothers breweries burned in unrelated fires—the first in 1963 and the second in 1964.

The Fitzgerald family had previously relocated from Troy to Glens Falls, New York, opening a beverage distribution company that is still in operation today.

The Microbrewing Movement and Bill Newman

With the closing of Schaefer in 1972, the Upper Hudson Valley was without a brewery for the first time in nearly 350 years, but this dry spell did not last long. Due to the early appearance of craft brewing, Albany's gap in local beer was no more than a decade

A new trend in American brewing was developing on the West Coast. The movement, in which entrepreneurs began opening small brewing facilities, began with the purchase and retooling of San Francisco's Anchor Brewery by Fritz Maytag in 1965 and continued into the 1970s with small independent breweries like New Albion opening in California in 1976 and Colorado's Boulder Beer Company, opening in 1979. Far smaller than even the smallest regional breweries, these "boutique breweries," as they were often called, had the capacity to produce only a fraction of what more established breweries could manage. However, these tiny ten- and fifteen-barrel brewing systems allowed the boutique brewer to expand on the idea of what American beer was. Darker hued ales, many inspired by traditional beer brewed in the United Kingdom, especially those with a pronounced hop flavor and aroma, became the hallmark of the early American craft beer.

Initially, the microbrewery was a phenomenon seen only on the West Coast and Colorado. In Albany, though, Bill Newman, an examiner for the New York State Division of the Budget with no brewing experience, was becoming increasingly interested in British-style, naturally conditioned "real ale" and saw an opportunity to bring that kind of beer to the East Coast. Bill knew of the city's vast brewing history and approached the city's government with that information as an incentive for investment. By 1979, Newman was capitalized with a $250,000 initial investment, provided by a local bank and state and local business development corporations.

Although Newman had acquired the capital to begin his brewery, he still had no experience brewing. A trip to the United Kingdom would change that. He spent three months under the tutelage of the father of the British independent brewery movement, Peter Austin, at his Ringwood Brewery

Above: William "Bill" Newman can be considered the grandfather of East Coast craft brewing. Newman opened his small brewery in 1980 in Albany, making it the first microbrewery to open east of the Rocky Mountains and the first new brewery to open in the Upper Hudson Valley since the end of the nineteenth century. *Courtesy of William S. Newman.*

Opposite: Bill Newman filling "Golden Gate" kegs—many of which were purchased from Anheuser-Busch. *Courtesy of William S. Newman.*

in Hampshire, England. With Austin, Newman received a crash course in all things brewing and toured many of the country's breweries—both big and small. He returned to Albany with plans for his own version of Austin's ten-barrel, open-fermenting brewing system, and within a year, Newman had the system built from scratch by a metal fabricator in Schenectady. He opened the William S. Newman Brewing Company in a building that had been used as keg storage by Schaefer on Learned Street in Albany. He soon was brewing the first of what would later be called "craft" beer on the East Coast, Albany Amber.

The microbrewing industry in the early 1980s was a lonely business. Resources, equipment and expertise were few and far between, especially on the East Coast. Newman was lucky early on, however, to have an affable

relationship with his rather large competitors—Anheuser-Busch. Whereas the relationship between Anheuser-Busch and many modern craft breweries might be seen as contentious today, in the early 1980s, the relationship was quite different, so much so that August "Auggie" Busch himself agreed to sell Newman a cache of the brewery's "Golden Gate" kegs when it switched from the bulbous bodied vessel to the modern straight-sided Sankey keg. They were

ideal for Newman's cask-conditioned ale. The brewing behemoth also agreed to sell two bushels of Fuggle hops, essential to Newman's British-style brews, to the tiny brewery, even after having bought ten years of futures in the crop.

By the mid-1980s, Newman's beer had amassed a small but loyal following in Albany, the Upper Hudson and the Northeast. He expanded his line to

Above: Michael Jackson (center), the noted British beer writer, visited Newman's brewery in 1985, saying, "If Newman succeeds in his heroic venture, he will undoubtedly inspire many others." *Courtesy of William S. Newman.*

Opposite: Newman showing his "Ale Cube" during the mid-1980s. *Courtesy of William S. Newman.*

include a Winter Ale and garnered awards at beer tastings and festivals like the Great American Beer Festival in Denver. Although Newman had initially focused on keg sales, the demand for his beer led to a rather unique packaging alternative prompted by Neil Golub, owner of the Price Chopper supermarket chain. Golub had inquired about carrying Newman's beer in his stores in bottles rather than kegs. Not having a bottling line, Newman improvised and purchased plastic water containers at a local camping store. The small jugs could be collapsed easily to expel air, keeping the beer fresh, were portable and could be refilled like a growler. Packaged in a cardboard box with a label, these plastic casks were dubbed "ale cubes" by those who bought them.

From his brewery's inception, Newman saw the possibility to disseminate his knowledge of microbrewing and opening a small brewery. He felt it imperative to pass along what he had learned from Peter Austin and his own experience to the second generation of microbrewers slowly filling the ranks of the new movement. Newman began holding start-up and brewing seminars at the brewery; he began teaching young brewers like Jim Patton, who would open Louisiana's Abita Brewing Company, Mark Stutrud of Summit Brewing in St. Paul Minnesota and, most notably, Jim Koch the founder of Boston Beer Company and the Samuel Adams brand.

Although Newman's beer was growing in popularity, the reality and expense of maintaining and operating a full-production brewery began to become apparent. Even with the additional income from his seminars, it became obvious that Newman needed to reorganize his business. In 1987, Newman closed his Albany brewery—the last production brewery to operate in the city—leasing the equipment to the fledgling Boston Beer Company. While his brick-and-mortar brewery had closed, he continued to brew, taking advantage of a new business model—that of a contract brewer.

Essentially, contact brewers operate in one of two ways: they either rent space, time and storage at an existing brewery, or they simply pay an existing brewery to make, and sometimes package, their particular recipe. In the late 1980s and early 1990s, contract brewing became an advantageous pact between small start-up microbreweries without the resources to open a full facility—or those who had exceeded capacity—and larger regional breweries who could bolster profits, shielding themselves from the ever increasing threat of buy-out and acquisition from large midwestern and international brewing corporations. It might even be said that contract brewing saved small and regional brewing in the United States.

Newman capitalized on this new trend, contracting first with Hibernia Brewery in Eau Claire, Wisconsin, then Schmidt, F.X. Matt and finally Catamount in Vermont. He also reinvigorated his product line, moving away from English-style ales to lager. He introduced a Dortmunder-style helles, dubbed Newman's Saratoga Lager, and reinvented his Albany Amber as a copper-hued märzen. These new partnerships also allowed Newman to bottle his beer for the first time. Most of Newman's contract brewing was done at F.X. Matt, a brewery that Newman had a long relationship with. Newman said of its owner:

> *F.X. was very good to us. I remember in 1983, I was still a very raw, young brewer, in my thirties and I got an invitation from the Master Brewers Association of the Western District of New York…and we met at Matt's, and they invited me to speak to them about boutique breweries. I was nervous as shit! I had not met F.X. Matt…he was very welcoming and gracious to a guy who was in his early thirties who knew shit about making beer!*

Bill Newman in the C.H. Evans brew house in 2014. *Photo by Craig Gravina.*

Unfortunately, even under the new contract model, Bill Newman saw the writing on the wall. Distribution issues and a failed business partnership had put a financial strain on the business, but even more so, while the craft beer industry was growing in leaps and bounds, those companies that had been infused with hundreds of thousands of dollars early on in their histories were growing even faster. California brands like Sierra Nevada and Pete's Wicked Ale were expanding into the East Coast markets, while the Boston Beer Company was beginning its meteoric rise as the dominant

East Coast craft brewery, as well. By 1993, Newman simply could no longer compete. Thinking of the future of his family, Bill Newman ended his career as a brewer.

1990 TO TODAY

As the 1980s became the 1990s, the concept of craft beer began to expand, and a new phenomenon arose—restaurants began offering beer made on premises alongside their food items. The brewpub had been born. Between 1990 and 2000, six brewpubs opened in the Upper Hudson Valley—Brown & Moran in Troy in 1993; the Original Saratoga Pub & Brewery in Saratoga Springs in 1995; Malt River Brewing Company in Latham, New York, in 1996; the Big House Brewing Company and Big House Grill in Albany in 1996 and 1999, respectively; and C.H. Evans at the Albany Pump Station in 1999.

As tenuous as opening a restaurant is, opening a restaurant/brewery has even more potential for failure—and fail is exactly what the majority of those original brewpubs did. The unwritten rule is that brewpubs will succeed on their food rather than their beer, and while most produced fairly popular beers, bad business practices and bad food would be their undoing. By 2004, four of the original six had closed—both Big House entities, as well as Malt River and the Original Saratoga Pub and Brewery.

Despite these closures, there have also been great successes. Garrett and Kelly Brown opened Brown & Moran, now Brown's Brewing Co. and weathered the early days of the brewpub craze. Brown's became an anchor business in the redevelopment and regentrification of downtown Troy and eventually grew into the biggest brewpub in New York State. Most recently, Brown's opened a second facility in North Hoosick, the Wallomsac Brewery, capable of twenty thousand barrels per year. The new brewery is located in what was once a nineteenth-century wallpaper mill along the Wallomsac River. The brewery is operational; however, Brown is still in the process of renovating the 150-plus-year-old factory.

Neil Evans, owner of C.H. Evans's Brewing Company at the Albany Pump Station, has revived and revitalized his own family's brewing heritage. Neil is a direct relative of the Hudson, New York Evans family and that city's Evans Brewery. As Albany's only brewpub, it continues to be one of the city's most popular restaurants. Both Brown's and C.H. Evans have won numerous

When Garry Brown and his partners opened Brown & Moran's in 1993, it became the first brewpub in the Upper Hudson Valley. Although it has been known by a variety of names—the Troy Pub and Brewery and, most recently, Brown's Brewing Co.—the brewpub has become a staple of Troy nightlife and is the oldest brewpub still operating in the area. *Photo by Craig Gravina*.

awards and accolades at national and international beer competitions, such as the Great American Beer Festival and the World Beer Cup.

In recent years, a few additional brewpubs have opened in the Upper Hudson. In 2003, Keegan Ales opened in Kingston. Since then, Cave Mountain Brewing Company in Windham has opened and Crossroads Brewing Company in Athens in 2010. Most recently, in 2012, Druthers Brewing Company opened in Saratoga Springs and the Dutch Ale House in Saugerties added a three-barrel brewing system to its restaurant and bar. Keegan's and Crossroad tap handles are regularly seen on the towers of beer bars and pubs across the

Revitalizing the city's former water-pumping station, Evans installed a fifteen-barrel brewing system, utilizing the building's existing industrial crane. C.H. Evans Brewing Company at the Albany Pump Station is the only brewery currently operating in Albany. *Photo by Craig Gravina.*

region, and Druther's has become a hot spot—in a city of hot spots—due both its food and beer.

Compared to brewpubs, production breweries are a wholly different animal. Over the last thirty years, many cities in the United States have seen some of their favorite brewpubs develop into full-scale, production breweries, while others have seen home-brewers and entrepreneurs with enough pluck and capital to grow their five- and ten-gallon brewing kits into ten- and fifteen-barrel, or in many cases much larger, breweries. The Upper Hudson Valley, unfortunately, hadn't seen this kind of brewery growth until recently. Prior to 2005, only two commercial breweries had opened since Bill Newman's operation closed in 1987. Since 2010, however, the area is becoming a new haven of micro-, nano- and even sub-nano craft breweries.

One production brewery, the Olde Saratoga Brewing Company, started as what was intended to be the East Coast extension of Portland, Oregon's Nor'Wester Brewery. Nor'Wester's principal owner, Jim Braneau, was struggling to secure financing for his ambitious one-hundred-barrel system being built in Saratoga Springs and approached the Indian industrialist Vijay Mallya, chairman of the Indian brewing conglomerate United Breweries International (UBI). A deal was struck, and the new facility—dubbed the North Country Brewery—was set as collateral. Mallya had been expanding UBI's influence in the American market, infusing cash into not only Braneus holdings but also three California breweries—Hopland, Humbolt and Arcta Brewing Companies. Ultimately, Braneau defaulted on his loan, and UBI acquired the Saratoga-based brewery. At nearly the same time, Mallaya acquired majority control of the Hopland Brewery in Mendocino, California, and changed that brewery's name to Mendocino Brewing Company.

Rather than an extension of Nor'Wester Brewery, the North Country Brewery opened in 1997 as the Olde Saratoga Brewing Company (a DBA of Releta Brewing Company LLC) as an adjunct of United Breweries. Today, Olde Saratoga operates, for all intents and purposes, as a satellite brewery for UBI's Kingfisher Line—billed as the world's bestselling Indian beer—and Mendocino's main line of beers. The brewery also brews under contract with a number of rotating breweries from across the Northeast, such as Long Island's Southampton Brewing Company and Cape Ann Brewing Company in Glouster, Massachusetts.

The journey to bring Shmaltz Brewing Company to the Upper Hudson Valley is as much of a cross-country romp as was Olde Saratoga. As was mentioned earlier, both breweries have roots in contact brewing, but whereas Old Saratoga acts as the contractor, Shmaltz, for the majority of its existence, was a contractee—and therefore had no official brewery.

Shmaltz's history starts in 1996 on the West Coast, when owner Jeremy Cown developed his HE'BREW line of beer from a home-brew recipe. Initially, Cowan self-distributed, but as his beer grew in popularity, he contracted with Anderson Valley Brewing, which helped him to expand distribution from California to the Midwest and eventually the East Coast. In 2003, Shmaltz moved production from the West Coast to New York at Olde Saratoga.

Shmaltz's HE'BREW series takes its theme from the Jewish faith, but Cowan puts an irreverent twist on the theology, having fun with Judaism with names like Messiah Bold and Jewbelation. In 2008, Shmaltz expanded its production and developed its Coney Island Lagers, a series of beers themed after the famous amusement park in Brooklyn, New York. A portion of the profits from this line benefited Coney Island USA, a

A sample from Shmaltz's lineup. *Photo by Craig Gravina.*

nonprofit arts organization preserving the history of the American carnival and boardwalk culture.

In 2012, however, Shmaltz made its biggest change yet. Stepping away from the contract-brewing methodology, Cowan opened a fifty-barrel brewery in Clifton Park, New York, a northern suburb of Albany. Deanna Fox, an Albany-area freelance writer and blogger, asked Cowan what brought Shmaltz to the Clifton Park area in July 2012. Cowan's answer was simple: "We have a bunch of staff that live here in the region, and it's been an incredible time for great craft beer in Upstate New York, as well as pretty much the rest of the state. This is an incredible opportunity to reach people who are halfway between New York City and Canada, and Boston and Syracuse."

Later that same year, it was announced that Shmaltz sold its Coney Island line to Alchemy & Science, a subsidiary of the Boston Beer Company, based out of Burlington, Vermont. The deal had a reported value of $2.9 million dollars.

Following Shmaltz's and Olde Saratoga's leads, a third brewery, Steadfast Beer Company, also has adopted a contract model. Although headquartered in Albany, Steadfast contracts with Paper City Brewing in Holyoke, Massachusetts, to produce its beer. Steadfast's beer, it must be said, is a bit unusual, although the style is becoming increasingly more common. Steadfast produces gluten-free beer, which uses sorghum rather than wheat or barley as its main fermentable. The brainchildren of this alternative brewery, Mark Crisafulli and Jeremy Hosier, own and manage two of the capital region's best-known beer stores, Oliver's Beverage and Westmere Beverage Centers, and have brought twenty-five years of beer-related experience to the idea of making beer for those people with gluten allergies and intolerance. Crisafulli said in a 2011 interview about many of the bland, gluten-free beers already on the market, "They're almost undrinkable—like Coors Light without the taste and without carbonation…If you have celiac disease, and are used to drinking good beer, there's nothing out there for you."

Steadfast aims to change that, having produced its first beer at Paper City in October 2011—a 6.8 percent pale ale. It has since released a Belgian-inspired golden ale, a seasonal pumpkin spice beer and a bier de garde to commemorate its second anniversary.

There are a few exceptions to the rule of Upper Hudson Valley breweries not springing-up from the ranks of the home-brew world. The first is Chatham Brewing, in the Columbia County, New York hill town of Chatham. The brewery was opened by Tom Cromwell, his partner Jake Cunningham and and former partner Chris Feronne. It began in a back-alley garage of Chatham's picturesque Main Street. Their good fortune was largely due to someone else's failure. In the right place at the right time, the principals of Chatham Brewing were able to purchase the former Big House Grill's three-barrel equipment when it went on the auction block for pennies on the dollar in 2007.

Chatham is a classic upstate New York bedroom community, its rural charm and small-town lifestyle lure Manhattanites away from the hustle and bustle of city living. Taking advantage of the village's summer and weekend residents, Chatham focused the majority of its sales on the New York City market, while also supplying a few pubs and restaurants in its immediate area. Over the course of the next six years, Chatham continued to gain popularity. The brewery was doing so well for itself that an expansion was begun in 2013 to include a storefront and tasting room, bringing the brewery's capacity to eighty barrels per week. The brewery has not been without setbacks, however. A late-night electrical fire at the brewery in July 2013 temporarily halted the expansion. Cromwell and Cunningham were undeterred. Within four days of the fire, growlers were being filled and kegs delivered.

Ten years ago, the primary school of thought was that, in order to be successful, a brewery needed minimally a ten-barrel brewing system, though fifteen was ideal. The main reasoning behind this was twofold. Larger systems require less brew days to reach demand; therefore, they were seen as more efficient and cost effective. Secondly, it was felt that expanding from a ten-barrel system to a larger set-up was a less expensive retro-fit. In the past five years, however, the nanobrewery concept has flown in the face of previous convention. One-, two- and three-barrel breweries have begun opening across the country, and the Upper Hudson Valley is no exception.

The Beer Diviner in Stephentown and Honey Hollow Brewery in Earlton are the area's first nanobreweries. Former State University of New York at Albany English professor Jonathan Prost opened his two-barrel brewery after an edifying trip to West Africa. On this trip, the professor was anointed as the "beer diviner" by a group of elders in the village of Dano—hence the name of his brewery. Whereas the Beer Diviner is small, Matty Taormina's Honey Hollow Brewery borders on the absurd. As a "sub-nano" brewer, Taormina operates a three-quarter barrel—a mere twenty-seven-gallon—brewing system.

Uniquely, both breweries were the first to be awarded New York State's Farm Brewery Licenses. Instituted by Governor Andrew Cuomo's administration in 2012 and 2013, Farm Brewery Licenses encourage breweries and brewpubs to use locally or state-sourced hops and fermentables in their products through tax incentives, as well as supports farmers within the state in growing those ingredients. To qualify for the license, brewers must comply with a determined set of percentages of raw ingredients to be used in each batch of beer. Currently, the bar is set at 20 percent New York–grown hops and 20 percent New York–sourced fermentables. Those percentages are set to increase incrementally over the next ten years. The licenses help not only to bolster New York's brewing industry but also to expand the state's agricultural base. At the time of this book's publication, there are fourteen Farm Breweries in New York, three of which are in the Upper Hudson Valley—the two previously mentioned and Brown's Brewing Co. in Troy.

The last twenty-five years have seen an amazing change in beer and brewing in the Upper Hudson Valley. The bleak days of 1989 and 1990 have blossomed into something of a beer renaissance. Although brewing in the Upper Hudson Valley has drastically declined since the turn of the twentieth century, in recent years there has been a resurgence of brewing in the area. It seems as though microbreweries, brewpubs and nanobreweries

The Beer Diviner's African inspiration is reflected in the brewery's label graphics. *Photo by Craig Gravina.*

are opening everyday—and those that have been operating already for years, like Brown's, are expanding. It's most likely that by the time this book has been published, the area will have seen the opening of a few more breweries up and down the river.

At the same time, while the brewing industry in Upper Hudson Valley is seeing a rebirth, it's also seeing an ever-increasing expansion of craft beer bars. This trend started twenty years ago with the opening of Mahar's Public House, a pub geared toward British-style ale, on upper Madison Avenue in Albany. Then came the gem of Lark Street—the Lionheart Pub—followed by City Beer Hall. In Schenectady, the Bier Abbey and Centre Street Pub offer some of the best craft beer in the area. The Ruck in Troy transformed itself from a college rugby bar to a craft beer destination and hosts local home-brew club meetings. Most uniquely, the Spotty Dog Books & Ale, a bookseller in Hudson, offers—along with its books—a variety of craft beers. Today, almost every town in the Upper Hudson Valley has at least one place to find great beer.

6
CONCLUSION

The year of this book's publication, 2014, marks the 400th anniversary of Fort Nassau, the first Dutch settlement in North America. From the beginning, beer was a hallmark of the Upper Hudson Valley. Within a few short years, it had grown from small, bubbling pots over hot coals to a major economic force. It helped to grow the small fur-trading outpost of Beverwijck, into the modern and industrialized city of Albany. It made fortunes and expanded influence. Beer was as essential to the growth and prosperity of the Upper Hudson Valley as steel was to Pittsburgh and the automobile was to Detroit.

And yet, the history of Upper Hudson and Albany brewing has been largely forgotten. In fact, the story of brewing in America is very much a "to the victor go the spoils" scenario. Although the nineteenth-century brewers of the Upper Hudson Valley were magnates in the very sense of the word—and their breweries were monolithic representations of their wealth and power—westward expansion, technological advancement and eventually governmental restriction stripped them of their previous glory, leaving a void to be filled with the history of those who survived and adapted best to those changes.

While the Upper Hudson Valley's brewing history has been overlooked, it has not been totally erased. There has been resurgence in New York—an effort to return to the state's brewing heritage. Small family farms that five years ago may have collapsed, unable to compete with large subsidized farming corporations, have turned to hop growing—many cultivating plants that grow wild along hedgerows and fences, feral cousins of central New York's booming nineteenth-century hop industry. Efforts to perfect New York–compatible barley are underway at the state's agriculture schools, like Cornell University, encouraging a rebirth of the malting industry within the state. These efforts harken back to the early nineteenth century, a point at which the Upper Hudson Valley was to enter into what would become the golden age of brewing for the area.

A number of cities and areas have taken up the mantle as the brewing "hub" or "capital" of the United States—St. Louis, Milwaukee, Vermont, the Pacific Northwest and northern California. Each one of them has contributed, in its own way, a piece of the puzzle that is American brewing. And though these cities or regions have earned the right to hold the title, none has offered so much over so long a period of time as the Upper Hudson Valley.

So, what can we take away from these past four hundred years?

Simply that the Upper Hudson Valley owes much of what it is today to beer and that American beer would have never been what it is—macro, micro, craft, nano or otherwise—had it not been for the Upper Hudson Valley.

7

A Beer and Brewery Tour

Most of the historic beer spots and breweries in the Upper Hudson Valley have been lost to the ages; however, their locations and lingering structures can still give us a peek into the area's beery heritage. Here is where some of them can be found.

Seventeeth-Century Dutch Breweries

SUNY Administration Plaza, Albany

Lower Broadway was home to some of Beverwijck's earliest breweries. Dean Street, now a walkway between the "Old Post Office" building and the SUNY administration building, was the home to the Van Schaick brewery, and the park just south of that location was where Pieter Bronck had his brewery.

Gansevoort Brewery and Stanwix Hall

515 Broadway, Albany

The Gansevoort Brewery sat on what was first Haendlers, then Market Street and now Broadway in Albany for about 150 years. In 1805, the brewery was leveled to make way for the hotel Stanwix Hall, also owned by the Gansevoorts. Today, the site is an office complex.

KING'S ARM INN

Greene and Beaver Streets, Albany

The inn that was the scene of that 1776 barroom brawl between Loyalist Tories and Revolutionary Patriots is long gone. The street corner where it sat, however, is still there. Located behind the U.S. Postal Service depot near the Holiday Inn Express, the forgotten crossroad still shows its original horse-cart street width. When standing there, turn to look east: the curve of the street mirrors the arc of the original fort walls from almost four hundred years ago.

BOYD BREWERY/ALBANY BREWING COMPANY

South Pearl and Green Streets, Albany

The long-gone Boyd Brewery (and later the Albany Brewing Co.) was located where the parking lot of the Albany County Department of Health and the Albany branch of the New York State Department of Motor Vehicles are today. The historic buildings along South Ferry Street are part of Albany's Pastures neighborhood. The neighborhood and the brewery developed out of Albany's post-Revolution growth and were the first expansion outside the city's stockade during the 1780s and '90s.

KIRK BREWERY/SMYTH & WALKER/FORT ORANGE BREWING COMPANY

904 Broadway, Albany

Andrew Kirk's north end brewery opened in the early 1830s and operated throughout most of the nineteenth and into the twentieth century. The building that stands today was most likely not built by Kirk. Its Dutch Revival style is more in line with late nineteenth-century architecture and may have been built as part of Smyth & Walker, a later brewery, at the same location. Today, the building is Stout, a popular Irish-themed bar. The alley to the left of the building is still named Kirk Way.

HOUCK'S CORNER TAVERN

Corner of Feura Bush and Elm Avenues, Bethlehem

Sitting at a crossroad to the southwest of Albany, the Houck's Corner Tavern was built around 1845. Albany Ale was likely served here, as well as in taverns like this up and down the Hudson River Valley. The white, Federal-style building still stands today as a residence rather than a tavern.

AMSDELL BROTHERS BREWERY

175 Jay Street, Albany

The Amsdell Brewery building opened as originally the White Malt House and Brewery and still stands today on the corner or Jay and Dove Streets in Albany's Center Square neighborhood. After the brewery closed, the main brewery was converted first into a hotel and then, shortly thereafter, into apartments, now known as the Knickerbocker Apartments. A portion of the brewery, which still faces Lancaster Street, was converted into a parking garage.

TAYLOR & SONS BREWERY

139 Broadway, Albany

After the Taylor Brewery burned in 1914, the Albany Iron and Hardware Company bought the lot and built a new building in nearly the exact same footprint as the brewery—in both square footage and height. Today, although not Taylor's original structure, the building is a good indication of the enormity of his operation.

CENTRE STREET BREWERY

308 Union Street, Schenectady

The location where Albert Schinnerer opened his brewery—at the intersection of Union and Centre Streets (now Broadway)—in Schenectady during the 1860s has revitalized its beer tradition. Opened in 2013, the Centre Street Pub (named in honor of the location's past) is a craft beer bar, beer garden and restaurant.

T.D. COLEMAN BROTHERS BREWERY

138–170 Chestnut Street, Albany

Opened in 1869, Coleman Brothers brewed ale on Chestnut Street in what is now Albany's Center Square neighborhood until the 1890s. The brewery was razed and replaced by fourteen row houses intended for young couples, known then as Bride's Row. Those row houses can still be seen close to the intersection of Chestnut and Lark Streets.

HINCKEL BREWERY

201 Park Avenue, Albany

In 1880, Frederick Hinckle built a brick brewery to replace his original wooden structure, which originally sat on this lot. The new structure operated at the corner of Park Avenue and Swan Streets until Prohibition and is the only complete brewery complex still standing in Albany. After Prohibition, the building was occupied by City Ice & Fuel Company, and in the early 1990s, the compound was regentrified and converted into apartments.

Fitzgerald Brothers Brewery

500 River Street, Troy

A municipal parking lot adjacent to the Hudson River on River Street in Troy, now occupies the location of the main brewery buildings of Fitzgerald Brothers, destroyed by fire in the 1960s. However, directly across on the east side of River Street a few buildings remain—remnants of the brewery's bottling department—now self-storage and a truck rental franchise.

Quinn & Nolan and Beverwyck/Schaefer Brewing Co.

48 North Ferry Street, Albany

James Quinn erected his brewery on North Ferry Street in 1845. Michael Nolan built his brewery, Beverwyck, next door to the older brewery in 1878. By 1950, the entire complex was purchased by F&M Schaefer Company. The vestigial remains of all three breweries can still be seen when North Ferry meets Erie Boulevard. What stands today is the former Schaefer cannery, where Quinn & Nolan once stood. To the right, across the railroad tracks was where Beverwyck was located.

Selected Bibliography

America's Historical Newspaper Database. New York State, various newspapers, 1733–1922.

Anderson, G.B. *Landmarks of Rensselaer County New York*. Syracuse, NY: D. Mason & Co., 1897.

Bachman, V.C. *Peltries or Plantations: The Economic Policies of the Dutch West India Company in New Netherland, 1623–1639*. Baltimore, MD: Johns Hopkins Press, 1969.

Bailey, F., and A. Green. *Wicked Albany Lawlessness & Liquor in the Prohibition Era*. Charleston, SC: The History Press, 2009.

Bryson, L. *New York Breweries*. Mechanicsburg, PA: Stackpole Books, 2003.

Bureau for Historical Services, Department of Human Resources City of Albany. *The Brewing Industry in 19th Century Albany*. Prepared by N. Gutkoska, 1974.

The Colonial Laws of New York from the Year 1664 to the Revolution… Albany, NY: James B. Lyon, state printer, 1894.

Columbia County at the End of the Century. Published and edited under the auspices of the *Hudson Gazette*. Hudson, NY: Record Printing and Publishing Co., 1900.

Crary, D. "Diamond Is Forever." *Hudson Valley Magazine* (September 2002).

Fox, D. "Shmaltz Brewing Company Opens in Clifton Park." http://blog.timesunion.com/eatlocal/shmaltz-brewing-company-opens-in-clifton-park/1985/#13852101=0 (accessed July 08, 2013).

Gravina, C. Various blog posts, 2010–13. drinkdrank1.com.

Gray, B., and J. Savage. *Ale in Prose and Verse*. New York: Russell's American Steam Printing House, 1866.

Grondahl, P. *Mayor Erastus Corning, Albany Icon, Albany Enigma*. Albany: State University of New York Press, 2007.

Howell, G.R., and J. Munsell. *History of the County of Schenectady, N.Y., from 1662 to 1886*. New York: Munsell, 1886.

Howell, G.R., and Johnathan Tenney. *Bi-centennial History of County of Albany, 1609–1886*. Vol. 1–4. New York: Munsell, 1886–88.

Jacobs, J. *The Colony of New Netherland: A Dutch Settlement in Seventeenth-Century America*. Ithaca, NY: Cornell University Press, 2009.

JK's Miscellaneous Beer Pages website. https://sites.google.com/site/jesskidden/jk%27smisc.beerpages.

"John Stanton." Obituary. *American Brewers' Review* 31, no. 1 (1917): 207.

Kennedy, W. *O Albany! The Improbable City of Political Wizards, Fearless Ethnics, Spectacular Aristocrats, Splendid Nobodies, and Underrated Scoundrels*. New York: Viking Press, 1983.

Kenney, A. *The Gansevoorts of Albany*. Syracuse, NY: Syracuse University Press, 1969.

LeBrun, F. "Newman: Brewing Faith in Followers." *Times Union*, March 27, 1983.

Matson, C. *Merchants and Empire: Trading in Colonial New York*. Baltimore, MD: Johns Hopkins Press, 1998.

McLeod, A. Various blog posts, 2010–13. A Good Beer Blog, http://beerblog.genx40.com/tag/albanyale.

Munsell, J. *Annals of Albany*. Various volumes. Albany, NY: Munsell, 1849–59.

———. *Collections of the History of Albany, from Its Present Time, with Notices of Its Public Institutions and Biographical Sketches of Citizens Deceased*. Vol. 6. Albany, NY: Munsell, 1871.

Murlin, E.L. *The New York Red Book*. Albany, NY: James B. Lyons, 1898.

New York State Legislature. Senate. Documents of the Senate of the State of New York. 58th session. Vol. 2, no. 29–89. Albany, NY: Croswell, 1835.

O'Callaghan, E.B. *History of New Netherland; Or, New York Under the Dutch*. New York: Appleton, 1846.

One Hundred Years of Brewing. Chicago: H.S. Rich & Co., 1901.

Osternik, C., and W.G. Ritchie. "A History of the C.H. Evans Brewery." http://gossipsofrivertown.blogspot.com/ (accessed October 22, 2012).

The People of Colonial Albany website, www.nysm.nysed.gov/albany.

Pereira, J., M.D., F.R.S. and L.S. *A Treatise on Food and Diet: With Observations on the Dietetical Regimen Suited for Disordered States of the Digestive Organs; and an Account of the Dietaries of Some of the Principal Metropolitan and Other*

Establishments for Paupers, Lunatics, Criminals, Children, the Sick, &c. New York: Langley, 1843.

A Report of the Trail of the Case of John Taylor vs. Edward C. Delavan*: Prosecuted for Alleged Libel; Tried at the Albany Circuit, April, 1940; and Mr. Delavan's Correspondence With the Ex. Committee of the Albany City Temperance Society, &c.* Albany, NY: Hoffman, White & Visscher, 1840.

Robinson, B. "Hanging Out: Newman's Brewery." *Empire State Report* (April 1983): 56.

Robinson, F.S. *Machine Politics: A Study of Albany's O'Connells.* New Brunswick, NJ: Transaction Books/Rutgers University, 1977.

Trent, William P., and Benjamin W. Wells, eds. "Daniel Denton." In *Colonial Prose and Poetry.* Vol. 2, *The Beginnings of Americanism: 1650–1710.* New York: Thomas Y. Crowell & Co., 1901. Reprinted, Bartleby.com, 2010. http://www.bartleby.com/163/209.html.

Valentine, D.T. *Manual of the Corporation of the City of New York for...(1856).* New York: The Council, 1842–70, 443. Electronic reproduction, 1852–66, Columbia University Libraries, 2010.

Van Wieren, D.P. *American Breweries II.* West Point, NY: Eastern Coast Breweriana Association, 1995.

Venema, J. *Beverwijck: A Dutch Village on the American Frontier, 1652–1664.* Hilversum, the Netherlands: Uitgeverij Verloren; Albany: State University of New York Press, 2003.

Warshaw Collection of Business Americana. *The Empire State: Its Industries and Wealth; Also an Historical and Descriptive Review of the Industries and Wealth of the Principal Cities and Towns in Albany, Rensselaer, Saratoga, Schenectady, Columbus, Ulster, Dutchess, Orange, and Westchester Counties.* New York: American Publishing and Engraving Co., 1888.

Weise, A.J. *Troy's One Hundred Years, 1789–1889.* Troy, NY: William H. Young, 1891.

White, C. "Brief History of German Brewers in Albany." http://findingyourpast.blogspot.com (accessed November 08, 2013).

Wilson, J.Q. *Varieties of Police Behavior: The Management of Law & Order in Eight Communities.* Cambridge, MA: Harvard University Press, 1968.

INDEX

ABOUT THE AUTHORS

CRAIG GRAVINA is a world-class beer drinker who was so infatuated with the sudsy stuff he took to writing a blog about it. He stumbled across the brewing history of his hometown, Albany, New York, and the long-lost story of Albany ale. This discovery resulted in the Albany Ale Project, a collaboration that explores the roots of Ontario's New York Loyalist traditions through the lens of a beer glass. Along with history, he also writes about beer culture, the state of brewing and beer making in the United States and around the globe.

The only ones capable of keeping him checked into reality are his loving wife, Amy (who, incidentally, dislikes beer but still has to listen to him, anyway), and his wonderful children, ages seven and four. (Wait, what? OK, OK, seven and a half and four and a half.)

ALAN MCLEOD has been writing about beer for over a decade. He lives in Kingston, Ontario, with his family and practices law. Through his work he has explored the heritage and history of his corner of Ontario. Alan is one of the founders of the Albany Ale Project.